Spiritual Awakening Made Simple

How to see through the mist of the mind
to the peace of the here and now

Spiritual Awakening Made Simple

How to see through the mist of the mind
to the peace of the here and now

Andrew Seaton

BOOKS

Winchester, UK
Washington, USA

JOHN HUNT PUBLISHING

First published by O-Books, 2020
O-Books is an imprint of John Hunt Publishing Ltd., 3 East St., Alresford,
Hampshire SO24 9EE, UK
office@jhpbooks.com
www.johnhuntpublishing.com
www.o-books.com

For distributor details and how to order please visit the 'Ordering' section on our website.

Design: Stuart Davies

Disclaimer
The information in this book is for educational and supportive purposes only. No reference to well-known health disorders or conditions should be construed as either diagnosis or recommended treatment of such disorders or conditions. No information in this book should be considered a substitute for the care and advice of medical or mental health professionals. No warranties or guarantees relating to information in this book are expressed or implied by the author or the publisher. Neither the author nor the publisher is responsible for the reader's interpretation of this book's content, or for any of the reader's choices, actions or outcomes.

UK: Printed and bound by CPI Group (UK) Ltd, Croydon, CR0 4YY
US: Printed and bound by Thomson-Shore, 7300 West Joy Road, Dexter, MI 48130

We operate a distinctive and ethical publishing philosophy in all areas of our business, from our global network of authors to production and worldwide distribution.

Contents

The only freedom is freedom from the known.
Jiddu Krishnamurti

A political orator wittily compared our party promises to western roads, which opened stately enough, with planted trees on either side, to tempt the traveller, but soon became narrow and narrower, and ended in a squirrel-track, and ran up a tree. So does culture with us; it ends in headache... Do not craze yourself with thinking, but go about your business anywhere. Life is not intellectual or critical, but sturdy.
Ralph Waldo Emerson

If the doors of perception were cleansed, everything would appear to man as it is, infinite.
William Blake

Preface

From time to time during my life, I have experienced dreams of guidance and what my future holds. I will relate a couple of brief examples. When I was 30, a friend asked me if I had ever asked for spiritual guidance in my dreams. The idea had never occurred to me. That night, before bed, I asked to be shown if there was anything important for me to add to my life or let go from my life for my highest good.

For the previous ten years, I had been a dedicated practitioner of a meditation technique that had been brought to the West by an Indian guru. That night, I dreamed that this guru was coming out of a private room and was caught off guard with a cigarette in his hand. Whoa! That was huge! Shaken but not stirred by this dream, I continued my meditation practice the following day. The next night, I dreamed that this guru said to me directly, "(This meditation technique) will not take you where you want to go." Whoa! I was more shaken, but I continued my meditation practice the following day. The third night in a row, I had a similar dream about this guru and meditation technique, the details of which I can't recall 34 years later. I stopped my meditation practice from that day on.

In a second example of dreams of guidance, in the early 1990s I dreamed that I was waiting in a queue, and a voice said to me, "You need to do further study, about how the mind works." Over the following 12 or so years, on and off, I did do a lot more study into the nature of human learning, knowledge and intelligence, and I discovered a surprising thing. What we think we know with our minds is not at all the reliable copy of reality that it is commonly assumed to be. Even more surprising was the discovery that all the peace, joy, love and creativity that people could want are closer than we ever imagine. They are our very nature, merely veiled by what we think we know.

I have recently experienced major changes in my consciousness and way of being in the world. Throughout 2017 and 2018, I was very focused on living the insights and practices I describe in this book. For most of 2018, I found myself living a very quiet life, and I experienced a flood of dreams about my spiritual awakening and about soon assisting others with awakening. In that year, I recorded more than four hundred such dreams. On September 23, six days after my sixty-fourth birthday, my spiritual awakening began in earnest.

In one of the dreams I had that night, I was standing in the middle of the sloped auditorium of a small theater. One after another, five or six groups of two or three male voices sang, "Who are you?" in beautiful, heavenly harmonies, a cappella, from different parts of the auditorium. Some groups were tenor pitch, others a bit lower, and the last was bass voices. The dream didn't need any interpretation. My awakening was beginning. Following the dream, energy began to move in my body and to shake it intermittently for about half an hour.

I have wanted to write this book for quite a while, but I could not ignore the feeling, dreams and messages that said, "Not yet." One time, early in 2018, I tried. I wrote down some key things I wanted to say on different sheets of paper which could become different chapters, and I lay them out on a table. Nothing would flow. I could not write the book from my mind. So, I accepted that life wanted me in downtime a while longer.

Then, in January of 2019, I came across a list of "things most people learn too late in life." I thought it was clichéd and completely inadequate, and again I felt the impulse to write this book. I had some thoughts about whether it might still be too soon, whether I might not be ready, but this time I couldn't ignore the feeling, dreams and other messages that said, "Write it now!" As I began writing, I was surprised at how content was coming to me and flowing into the book. A week into writing, I experienced a strange sense. I looked back on the day's writing and felt, "What I have written couldn't have been different."

While the practices I write about in this book are described in my own way and with my own emphasis, different ones have been recommended by various teachers over the centuries, including Eckhart Tolle and Noah Elkrief, to name a couple of present-day ones. Many of the particulars I discuss have been spoken of before, by one teacher here or another there. And yet, there is an overwhelming amount of conceptual and practical clutter, error and confusion in the world regarding spirituality, and many people are feeling frustrated. Through my long, deep and broad investigations in this area, I have finally been able to see through the muddle and pull the essentials together in a way that has served my own awakening well. Through intuitive inspiration, I have been able to present them here in a concise, unified and practical formulation that many will find makes things clear and gives their awakening the traction they are wanting. I hope that you are one of those.

Andrew Seaton
January 2019

Introduction

Thank you for opening this book. I hope that in it you might find inspiration and practical guidance for a more peace-filled, spiritually conscious life.

I don't use the term "spiritually conscious" to suggest that you would benefit from being more aware of spiritual *concepts*. There are those who know little or nothing of spiritual concepts and yet are exceptionally spiritually conscious. On the other hand, many people who are very aware of spiritual concepts are quite unconscious, spiritually speaking. That would include most of humanity. I use the term spiritually conscious to refer to an awareness beyond the conceptual mind, beyond thinking.

The insights described in this book are broadly consistent with a huge body of wisdom expressed over thousands of years, particularly by people who have realized their inner nature. They are also consistent with many contemporary understandings about human functioning.

However, most of what has been written and spoken about peace, identity and human consciousness overlooks the simplicity of the insights and practices I describe and the potential immediacy of their realization in experience. That is due partly to the vastness of that body of understandings and the tendency of writers and teachers to be influenced by their particular biography and cultural context. Mostly, however, it is due to problems inherent in expressing in words and understanding with the mind aspects of human experience and consciousness which are beyond the conceptual mind.

One of the most influential philosophical statements of any era was made during the seventeenth century, when philosopher and scientist René Descartes famously declared, "I think, therefore I am." "But," he admitted, less famously, "I do not yet sufficiently understand what this 'I' is that now necessarily exists." His reasoning led him to conclude that all things, including the "I," are perceived "by the intellect alone."[1] What else could reasoning, alone, conclude?

Given the backdrop of oppressive religious authority at the time, even the advocacy of the limited authority of reason was a major step forward for humanity. Its consequence, however, was that since that time the emphasis of science, philosophy and education has been on conceptual analysis of the world through its fragmentation into simpler components in a search for certainty and control.[2]

Most adults in the world today have so lost touch with their inner awareness and have become so identified with the mind and conceptual knowledge that they confuse the spiritual dimension of life with the abstract, rational activity of thinking, talking and writing about philosophical, metaphysical and religious concepts. As a result, adults in general, and specialists in philosophy, psychology and education in particular, tend to neglect, deny and even repress the spiritual consciousness in themselves and others, including children.[3]

However, my research into the nature of learning, knowledge and behavior revealed that the tide has well and truly begun to turn. There is a large body of insights, in nearly every field, showing the inadequacy of popular assumptions about reality, knowledge and human nature. The old assumptions that we still see reflected in mainstream culture are merely cultural lag.

Around the world, there is a ground-swell of people, in all walks of life, questioning old structures, including conceptual structures, and exploring the deeper possibilities of human consciousness and experience. Behind the scenes, a new era is rapidly unfolding for humanity, in which forms and structures will no longer overshadow the formless dimension of life. This book is a contribution to this growing impulse to spiritual awakening.

I am well aware that in writing this book I myself am

attempting to use words to point you, the reader, to who you are beyond words and the mind. While the book necessarily involves some explaining, its purpose is to facilitate recognition and discovery, rather than to persuade you conceptually. More beliefs are not what is needed. As you read through the book, please take the time to do, experience and notice the things I suggest. Use the book as a practical manual for your awakening, rather than as merely another source of food for thought.

My style of expression tends to be fairly direct. At all times, however, the invitation is simply to ask yourself if what I have written rings a bell of recognition. Try to hold the ideas in this book lightly. Don't overthink them. We are leveraging language and the mind for our subtler purpose, but not wanting to get caught up in playing the mind's games. If there is something in the book for which you can't find an inner echo, please follow the advice I heard given by Patricia Sun many years ago, and put it on a mental shelf labeled "Maybe Wrong, Maybe Later."

Endnotes

1. Descartes 1996, para. 6, 18.
2. It is ironic that this intellectual search for certainty was given such impetus by Descartes, since his own intellectual search for certainty led him to conclude that the only "true thing" left is "Perhaps just the one fact that nothing is certain" (1996, para. 2).
3. See, for example, Hart 2003, pp. 4, 14.

Chapter 1

The Life You Are

The wisdom of many traditional and Eastern cultures, based on direct personal experiences, acknowledges our fundamental connectedness with all life. Black Elk, elder of the Oglala Sioux, for example, explained that:

> The first peace, which is the most important, is that which comes within the souls of men when they realize their relationship, their oneness, with the universe and all its Powers, and when they realize that at the center of the universe dwells Wakan-Tanka, and that this center is really everywhere, it is within each of us.[1]

The unchanging essence of life is everywhere, but hidden.

You are living your life in a world of form and change, but the essence of life is a formless organizing principle. It is not accessible to the senses or the intellect. It is infinite or spiritual, in the sense that it is subtler than the world of form. It flows through all creatures, all things, all situations, all happenings. It is the inner life within everything.

As the formless organizing principle within you, the essence of life is the essence of you. A drop of water is a uniquely individual manifestation, but its nature is the same as the ocean, rain, rivers, icebergs, steam and frost. A spark is an individual manifestation, but its nature is the same as the fire from which it came. You are an individual manifestation, but your essential nature, the real you, is the same formless organizing principle that flows through all life.

The essential reality of life is not the changing forms of the people, objects, situations and events of the material world, which are apparent to the senses. Nor is it the mental or emotional forms that each of us constructs. The inner organizing principle of life is formless.

The essential reality of you is subtler than your physical body, your mind and your emotions. You *have* a body, a mind and emotions. But you are not your body, not the contents or operations of your mind and not your emotions. These forms have changed during your life, but the essence of you has not changed.

When you were 10 years old, did you feel like you were you? Did you feel like you were you when you were 15? When you were 20? When you were 30? When you were 40? Do you feel like you are you, now? But, has your body changed? Are any beliefs different? Have your pleasures, concerns and roles changed?

You might have a memory of being happy at 10, unpopular at 15, uncertain about finding a partner at 20, not as financially well-off as you would like at 30 and wanting a divorce at 40 (to use some not uncommon examples). But beneath the thought, emotion or situation that you may recall, was there a sense that you were you, having that experience? You are the underlying awareness that has remained constant through your life, if mostly hidden.

Being Aware of Being Aware

The real you is formless awareness. You are not a thing. You are not a concept. As a result, your mind is not able to know the real you as an object. The essence of you is a subtler reality than your eyes are able to see or your intellect is able to fathom. You aren't able to know the essence of you. You *are* able to *be* it. You *are* it. You are formless consciousness, formless awareness.

Try not to get stuck on these words as you read them in this book. They will frustrate the intellect, because they point to something beyond the realm of the intellect. Relax the grip of your mind. Words can't capture, only point in the direction of the essential reality of you and all life. From time to time, I will suggest that you allow your awareness to come out of thinking, out of form, and back to formless awareness. You might like to try it now.

Soften your gaze. On an out breath, consciously let go and relax. Let your awareness be on the flow of your breath for a few moments, noting the sensation of air passing in and out of the nostrils. Now notice that you are the awareness noticing the sensation of air moving through your nostrils. In that space of quiet noticing, feel your aliveness.

That's it. For a few seconds at least, your attention came away from the contents of your mind, out of form, and into formless awareness, into Being, the essence of you and all life. As you read on, notice that you are the one noticing the reading taking place and the thoughts popping into your mind about what you are reading.

The essence of life is a formless organizing principle that interpenetrates every part of the world you live in. You are capable of being that formless awareness that is the inner reality of life, the intrinsic value of all things. You *are* that formless awareness. You are wholeness, completeness, everything. But human beings have the ability to be *conscious* expressions of that essence. You have ordinary waking consciousness, such as when you are aware of a bird or a thought or an emotion. But you also have the capability of conscious identity with the essence of life.

All things that truly matter to humans arise from the subtle depths of life: things like peace, beauty, joy, connectedness, intuition and playfulness. There are on the planet now and historically rare individuals who fully embody these qualities of consciousness. What is it that gets in the way of all people embodying those qualities? Why is it that most people have only sensed their connectedness with the essence of life occasionally, fleetingly, perhaps only dimly?

If your true identity is formless awareness, the spiritual organizing principle within all life, how did you come to lose sight of that? How did you come to feel incomplete? How did you come to feel troubled and dissatisfied? Let us look at just a few brief descriptions of awakened consciousness to see if we can get a hint as to why it has not been common.

The Requirement for Spiritual Awareness

Botanist and agricultural scientist Luther Burbank gave us a hint about the conditions and benefits of this connected mode of being, when he described them in this way:

> Preconceived notions, dogmas, and all personal prejudice and bias must be laid aside. Listen patiently, quietly, and reverently to the lessons, one by one, which Mother Nature has to teach, shedding light on that which was before a mystery, so that all who will, may see and know. She conveys her truths only to those who are passive and receptive. Accepting these truths as suggested, wherever they may lead, then we have the whole universe in harmony with us.[2]

Brain scientist Jill Bolte Taylor gained an unexpected insight into this question, when she had a stroke. The stroke was caused by a blood clot the size of a golf ball pressing against the language centers of her brain, effectively shutting down the left hemisphere.

> On the morning of the stroke, I woke up to a pounding pain behind my left eye...
> And I look down at my arm, and I realize that I can no longer define the boundaries of my body. I can't define where I begin and where I end, because the atoms and the molecules of my arm blended with the atoms and molecules of the wall. And all I could detect was this energy. Energy. And I'm asking

myself, "What is wrong with me? What is going on?" And in that moment, my brain chatter, my left hemisphere brain chatter, went totally silent. Just like someone took a remote control and pushed the mute button. Total silence.

And at first, I was shocked to find myself inside of a silent mind. But then I was immediately captivated by the magnificence of the energy around me. And because I could no longer identify the boundaries of my body, I felt enormous and expansive. I felt at one with all the energy that was, and it was beautiful there.[3]

It took Taylor eight years to fully recover from her stroke, but she treasures the liberating "stroke of insight" that her experience gave her. She explains:

My left hemisphere had been trained to perceive myself as a solid, separate from others. Now, released from that restrictive circuitry, my right hemisphere relished its attachment to the eternal flow. I was no longer isolated and alone. My soul was as big as the universe and frolicked with glee in a boundless sea.

...(T)here was both freedom and challenge for me in recognising that our perception of the external world, and our relationship to it, is a product of our neurological circuitry. For all those years of my life, I really had been a figment of my own imagination![4]

Eckhart Tolle had a somewhat similar experience of re-establishing awareness of self-as-connected-with-all-life. Unlike Taylor's, however, his experience arose out of a crisis of thought and emotion, rather than of the physical body. Tolle recalls:

One night... I woke up in the early hours with a feeling of absolute dread... (E)verything felt so alien, so hostile, and so utterly meaningless that it created in me a deep loathing of the world... (and of) my own existence...

"I cannot live with myself any longer." This was the thought that kept repeating itself in my mind. Then suddenly I became aware of what a peculiar thought it was. "Am I one or two? If I cannot live with myself, there must be two of me: the 'I' and the 'self' that 'I' cannot live with." "Maybe," I thought, "only one of them is real."

I was so stunned by this strange realization that my mind stopped. I was fully conscious, but there were no more thoughts. Then I felt drawn into what seemed like a vortex of energy...

(In the morning) ...I opened my eyes. The first light of dawn was filtering through the curtains. Without any thought, I felt, I knew, that there is infinitely more to light than we realize. That soft luminosity filtering through the curtains was love itself. Tears came into my eyes. I got up and walked around the room. I recognized the room, and yet I knew that I had never truly seen it before. Everything was fresh and pristine, as if it had just come into existence. I picked up things, a pencil, an empty bottle, marveling at the beauty and aliveness of it all.

...I could still function in the world, although I realized that nothing I ever *did* could possibly add anything to what I already had... More fundamental, perhaps, than any experience is the undercurrent of peace that has never left me since then.[5]

The awakening experience of plant pathologist Masanobu Fukuoka came after being in an agony of doubt about the nature of life and death. He described it as having great significance for others.

One night as I wandered, I collapsed in exhaustion on a hill overlooking the harbour, finally dozing against the trunk of a large tree... As the breeze blew up from below the bluff, the morning mist suddenly disappeared. Just at that moment a night heron appeared, gave a sharp cry, and flew away into the distance. I could hear the flapping of its wings. In an instant all my doubts and the gloomy mist of my confusion vanished. Everything I had held in firm conviction, everything upon which I had ordinarily relied was swept away with the wind. I felt that I understood just one thing. Without my thinking about them, words came from my mouth: "In this world there is nothing at all..." I felt that I understood nothing.

I could see that all the concepts to which I had been clinging, the very notion of existence itself, were empty fabrications. My spirit became light and clear. I was dancing wildly for joy... Everything that had possessed me, all the agonies, disappeared like dreams and illusions, and something one might call "true nature" stood revealed.

...(T)here is nothing special about me, but what I have glimpsed is vastly important.[6]

Just these few examples of awakened consciousness suggest two surprising things. The first is that what seems, more than anything else, to get in the way of our experiencing the immense peace and joy of connected consciousness is *what we think we know* with our conceptual mind.

In fact, many wisdom teachings warn us of the limitations and distortions of the rational processes of the mind. The *Lankavatara Sutra*, for example, explains that:

Those who vainly reason without understanding the truth are lost in the jungle of the Vijnanas (the various forms of relative knowledge), running about here and there and trying to justify their view of ego-substance.

The self realized in your inmost consciousness appears in

its purity; this... is not the realm of those given over to mere reasoning.[7]

And in the *Tao Te Ching*, Lao Tzu observes that:

The more you know,
the less you understand...
In the pursuit of knowledge,
every day something is added.
In the practice of the Tao,
every day something is dropped...
Can you step back from your own mind
and thus understand all things?[8]

Spiritual Awakening Is Natural

The second surprising thing suggested by the above few examples of direct awareness of oneness with all of life is that nothing could be more natural. Your "awareness Self" is already complete, already who you are. Spiritual awakening is not the result of fixing or improving yourself. The notion of spiritual "development" is a myth that can be a great hindrance.

Awakening occurs naturally as you give up on the interpreting and judging mind. It is not a case of becoming something that you are not, merely of letting go something that you are not. Like sliding down a slippery slide, awakening has its own inertia once you let go of ideas of who you are, what things mean and how things should be.

Peace, contentment and connectedness are our nature. It is perfectly natural that we should all be able to experience this awareness Self. And yet, many people aspiring to spiritual awakening have come to feel that it's too complicated, that it takes too long and their efforts aren't bearing much fruit. Some have lost heart. Many don't quite know what to believe out of so much that is written and spoken about spirituality. Many believe too much. Some wonder whether they deserve it. I hope that readers of this book will discover for themselves that these concerns are unnecessary.

Let us look more closely, then, at how it is that this most natural mode of consciousness has not been common, at why the mass of humanity lives, in varying degrees, in an alienated and discontented mode of being, dominated by an illusory sense of self-as-separate. Then, we will look at some simple and effective ways that the awareness of self-as-connected-with-all-life can become the conscious experience of many, or at least, if you feel drawn, how it can become *your* experience.

Endnotes

1. Black Elk 1988, p. 115.
2. Quoted in Buhner 2004, p. 155.
3. Taylor 2008a.
4. Taylor 2008b, pp. 69–70.
5. Tolle 2016, pp. 1–3.
6. Fukuoka 1978, pp. 8–10.
7. Quoted in Huxley 2004, p. 8.
8. Tzu 2013, Chaps. 47–48, 10.

Chapter 2

Your Idea of You and the World

(As you read on, don't read too quickly or voraciously. Notice that you are the awareness noticing that you are reading. Simply say to yourself, "I am the one noticing that I am reading." You may not be able to do that very clearly or for long. That doesn't matter. It is a valuable thing to do. That is spiritual awakening.)

We come into the world of form as a baby. William Wordsworth described it like this:

> *Our birth is but a sleep and a forgetting:*
> *The Soul that rises with us, our life's Star,*
> *Hath had elsewhere its setting,*
> *And cometh from afar:*
> *Not in entire forgetfulness,*
> *And not in utter nakedness,*
> *But trailing clouds of glory do we come*
> *From God, who is our home:*
> *Heaven lies about us in our infancy!*[1]

Soon, however, we gain a sense that we are separate from people and things around us, in a world of limits and change.

This new sense of self-as-separate is accompanied by a certain insecurity, a sense of incompleteness, an underlying fear. We want to get what we need from the world outside us, in order to feel safe, in order to feel satisfied. We gradually learn that thinking of ourselves as a separate entity and behaving in particular ways are essential to getting what we feel we lack.

In your early months and years, for example, you noticed that when you cried, you got attention and often a meal. Your attention was drawn outward, away from the awareness Self that you really are. You began to identify with your own form. Identification with the world of form, in general, caused you to forget who you really are.

The Mist of the Mind

In your early years, your sense of "me" and "mine" developed, and your body, mind and emotions became your identity. You formed an ego, by which I do not mean a sense of "I am the greatest," but a sense of self-as-separate, an *idea* of who you are, a conceptual identity.

You also became emotionally attached to certain experiences, people and things in the world of form around you. By "attached" I mean that you came to regard these things as a part of who you are, as essential to who you are. You would thenceforth feel a sense of loss or diminishment or insecurity, if they were to disappear from your life. A process of conditioning or programming had begun.

Each new bit of learning or conditioning you took on was not just a new word, concept, skill or habit. Innumerable researchers have concluded that each of these things is always only one inseparable facet of a subtle and complex network of goal-directed operating patterns, linked to previous experience. Each operating pattern involves many facets of your individuality, which work together in a dynamically integrated way. Each pattern involves an aim or desire, memory, perception, thought, emotion and action, as well as energy flows and biochemical processes throughout the body. While I may often refer in this book to thoughts, or to other particular facets of these conditioned operating patterns, bear in mind that *those facets don't ever stand alone.*

During childhood, you constructed a multitude of operating patterns concerning your identity, beliefs about people and the world, and expectations, as well as the behaviors most likely to earn rewards, avoid losses and penalties, and ensure your survival. From your earliest infancy, and even prenatally, you were strongly influenced by patterns of emotion, intent, language and behavior that you were involved with directly or perceived in your environment. Your operating patterns were formed and reinforced by your interpretations of your experience, particularly at home and at school. The formation of any new operating pattern was influenced by existing ones.

With each new operating pattern that you created, you concluded, in effect, not just that "This is the way it was just now," but that "This is the way it *is*." More than this, you came to conclude that "This is the way it *should* be" and that "It should not be any *other* way." Your thoughts and emotions began to take on a life of their own. They have constantly colored and judged your perceptions to confirm what you had come to believe about yourself and the world. You became emotionally attached to or identified with your interpretations of your experience. You lost awareness of your own beingness, of the awareness Self.

It is hugely liberating, if perhaps a little disconcerting at first, to realize that what each of us learned in our childhood about who we are and about the world around us is not a copy of reality. It is not true. We did not *acquire* knowledge-as-truth about ourselves and the world. We *constructed* ideas and stories in our minds and called them knowledge. We interpreted our experience through the mist or filter of our past experiences and our fears, needs, preferences and goals.

Even now, as adults, except for a small number of spiritually awakened individuals, people don't perceive the world-as-it-is. What you think you know about yourself and the world is the result of the conditioning you have experienced, based on your pre-programming, your personal experiences and the cultures you have been immersed in. Let us look at how your perception, or learning, is an activity of constructing meaning, rather than a registering of the world-as-it-is.

You Interpret What You Perceive

First, you *interpret* sensory input. Signals received by your physical senses represent the *intensity* of stimulation, but the *quality or nature* of the thing or event that causes the stimulation is not encoded.[2] The picture of the world that you construct from relationships between perceptual signals, including what you hear and read, is an *interpretation*. Understanding that we interpret what we perceive leads us to ask, "What determines the interpretation each of us gives to our perceptions?"

Around the middle of the twentieth century, it began to be quite widely acknowledged that observations and reports of raw data and facts are influenced by our conditioned operating patterns: our pre-existing assumptions, conceptual structures, language patterns, expectations, goals and preferences.[3] Philosopher of science Norwood Hanson gave an example from the history of science, when observation failed to resolve a dispute between Johannes Kepler and Tycho Brahe as to whether the Sun orbits the Earth or vice versa.[4] Brahe "saw" the Sun traveling from our eastern to western horizon, circling the fixed Earth. But Kepler "saw" the Earth's eastern horizon dipping or turning away from the fixed Sun. Each observer's perception had a different conceptual organization. The two different perceptions—that the Sun was orbiting the Earth and that the Earth was orbiting the Sun—were due to differences between what Brahe and Kepler *thought they knew*.

Hanson also illustrated this point by reference to several gestalt images, which are specifically designed so that alternative interpretations of the subject-matter are possible. One such image is of a bird, which could alternatively be seen to be an antelope. Perhaps the best-known image of this kind is the one that can appear to be either a young woman or an old woman. You may be familiar with it. William E. Hill drew a famous version of it, which he humorously titled *My Wife and My Mother-in-Law*.[5] The interesting thing about such images is that some people will first see a particular thing in the image, while other people will first see something quite different, even though the perceptual signals being received by each observer are the same.

If we were to say that such images are ambiguous or that they are optical illusions, we would be missing the point. Through the commonly different interpretations, such images serve to illustrate that ambiguity or illusion are *in each observer's conceptual structures, not in the image.* They highlight the fact that the conditioned mind adds a significance to *all* perceptions that is not inherent in the object of perception. What Person A makes a word, object, person, situation or experience mean may be quite different from what Person B makes it mean, or even from what Person A makes it mean when they are in a different context or frame of mind.

You Select What You Perceive

There is a second way in which sensory perception is a constructive activity, rather than a registering of the world-as-it-is. You select certain perceptions and not others, most often subconsciously. About ten years ago, I experienced a striking practical illustration of this phenomenon, when I watched a television science program called *Sleek Geeks*.

The studio audience and viewers at home were invited to watch a short video clip.[6] The clip showed two basketball teams, one dressed in black, the other in white, and each team had a basketball. As all the players mingled and moved quickly around each other, members of each team were passing their ball only to members of their own team. Viewers were asked to count how many times members of the white team passed their ball to each other.

Rising to the challenge, and determined to be right, I watched closely. I counted 24 passes. After showing the video, the program presenters asked members of the studio audience to reveal how many passes they had counted. Several raised their hands for 22. Several more for 23. Most hands were raised by those who had counted 24 passes. The presenters congratulated these people on observing the correct number of passes. I felt chuffed with pride at my acute powers of observation.

Then, one member of the studio audience said that he had seen a gorilla. The presenters showed their surprise, gently teased the person a little and asked if any others in the studio audience had seen a gorilla. None had. And if I knew one thing, it was that there had not been any gorilla. The presenters then replayed the video clip, emphasizing that it was the identical clip to the one just shown. Lo and behold! There, dancing around among the two teams of basketball players, was a person dressed in a black gorilla suit!

Like most people in the studio audience, I had been focused on counting and on the activity of things white. As a result, I had not consciously registered the presence of a shape which was both unexpected and black. Suddenly humbled, I smiled at such a dramatic illustration of how people perceive selectively, according to interest and expectation.

It is instructive, also, to turn this illustration upside down. What if the hosts of the show had *not* specified filtering criteria? What if they had not emphasized concentrating on players dressed in white or the process of counting? What if they had not put pride at stake by building it up as a kind of personal challenge: "Let's see how good you are at this!" If people had just been invited to watch the video clip with relaxed alertness, with no penalties or pay-offs at stake, most people would have seen the gorilla. It is not that human consciousness is incapable of seeing reality. It is the *conditioned mind* that is unable to perceive the world objectively, as it is in reality. It perceives through the filter of its attachments: its interests, fears and expectations.

This perceptual filtering is one of two main kinds of learning and knowing. Learning psychologist Jean Piaget referred to it as "assimilation." Assimilation means "treating new material *as an instance of something known,"* so that "when an organism assimilates, it remains unaware of, or disregards, whatever does not fit into the conceptual structures it possesses."[7] The conditioned mind is continually asking, "How is this new situation or input related to what I have experienced or accepted in the past?" We are selective in what we attend to, according to our assumptions and concerns.

A much rarer kind of learning requires some unlearning. It takes place when undeniable input causes a dismantling of an existing piece of knowledge, an existing operating pattern, and the possible construction of a new one.[8] An example is the culture shock which some people experience when first visiting a part of the world where the common ways of seeing and doing things are radically different from what they are used to. They are suddenly confronted with evidence that the ideas they have believed about themselves and the world are not a reflection of the way-things-are, but merely one of many possible ways of thinking about themselves and the world. Except in its most trivial manifestations, this type of learning is relatively rare. Learning that involves the kind of selective perception we saw in the gorilla example is far more usual.

The story of my not registering the presence of the gorilla is an example of remaining *unaware* of something that did not fit my expectations or interests. In the experience of culture shock, it is not possible to remain unaware of the input. Nevertheless, not all people who experience culture shock will experience a crumbling of their conditioned assumptions about themselves and the world. Many will go back home and mentally withdraw into the comfort of established operating patterns and conceptual structures by *disregarding* the input they received on their travels. "Thank God I am home!"

The deeper kind of learning, which involves the dismantling of some conditioned conceptual structures, will not take place if new information is not important to you. It won't take place if you don't think the new information is valid. And it won't take place if you don't see, or don't want to see, that new information shows an inadequacy in your existing knowledge or operating patterns. In the latter situation, people tend to close their minds, and strong emotions of resistance or hostility may be aroused. Conditioned ways of seeing ourselves and the world can be very resilient.

Here is an example of people filtering out some input by disregarding it, after having become aware of it. While I was working for a couple of years as an academic, I was contacted by a senior colleague and told that the university had a prospective fee-paying international student, who they might ask me to supervise. I was asked to review his application and make a recommendation regarding his suitability for undertaking doctoral research. The applicant was a Thai national, the son of a wealthy Thai politician. Let us call him Somchai.

Somchai had a recent master's degree, awarded by another Australian university, and I was provided with a copy of his thesis. It was very short, very superficial and included just two references. I considered the standard of scholarship to be similar to a reasonably good upper high school assignment. The assessor had graded it "B," had made a comment something like "Well done," and Somchai had been awarded his master's degree. The assessor's perceptual filter must have been something like, "I have commercial pressures on me to pass the thesis of this fee-paying international student."

I emailed my colleague and recommended that Somchai's application to be accepted into the doctoral program be declined, unless more satisfactory evidence could be provided that he had, or could develop, the required academic ability. A couple of weeks later, I received a message that Somchai's application had been accepted, and he would soon contact me as his doctoral research supervisor!

I was shocked at how different my colleague's perception of

the situation was from mine. My perceptual filter was, "Does the applicant have the required ability?" My colleague's perceptual filter must have been something like, "It's my job to recruit my quota of fee-paying international students to make money for the university." That driving concern enabled him to disregard input that he had received: both the evidence of inadequate ability provided by Somchai's master's thesis and my recommendation that his application be declined.[9]

Here is another example of how we frequently disregard input. Not so long ago, I saw a travel documentary about remote northeast India, near where it borders Myanmar. Prominent among the food delicacies available at the markets were huge spiders, grubs, rats, snakes and frogs. I watched two Westerners bravely eating fried grubs and a whole roasted rat.

I found it an interesting example of how the perceptual filtering regarding the foods we find appealing and the ones we find repulsive is largely a matter of conditioned attitudes. When I am in my garden or in wild nature, my perceptual filters cause me to disregard any spiders, grubs, rats, snakes and frogs as potential food sources. And yet, if I were lost in wild nature and starving, I see that the selection criteria operating in my perceptual filters would change to allow those things. (I am still not completely certain about that.)

A final example, even more simple and close to home. Most people who find dandelions growing in their garden perceive them as weeds. "What a nuisance!" When looking for food or medicine, they disregard them. Other people see dandelion as a valuable medicinal herb and salad green, and are delighted to find them growing wild in their garden. "What a bonus!" When looking for weeds to remove, they disregard dandelions. Individually and culturally selective perception is everywhere, all the time.

Such selective perception does not just occur in personal aspects of our daily life. Even scientists, who we most tend to think of as impartially basing their conclusions on all the reliable evidence before them, are selective in their perception. In practice, scientists often suppress unusual data, because it is subversive of the dominant theories and views of the day.[10] It is ignored, even hidden, because it inconveniently contradicts what they think they already know.

The Illusion of What You Think You Know

Perception is an interpretive and selective process, rather than a registering of the world-as-it-is. What we like to think of as "knowledge" is not a copy of reality, but merely an individual's abstract and fragmenting *construction* of reality. Such conceptual constructions can never reproduce the actuality of life-as-it-is. Conceptual knowledge cannot capture or reproduce the subtlety, truth, wholeness, thisness and livingness of reality.

There are at least two professions, education and science, in which we might assume that this insight would be widely understood and taught. Such is not the case. In the field of education, it is generally not noticed. It contradicts the current paradigm, the dominant assumptions and practices of education, which reflect a commodity view of knowledge-as-truth and a primary function of ranking people on their accumulation of it. For educators, it is another inconvenient truth. It is rarely acknowledged. If noticed, it is soon disregarded.

In science, likewise, there is only rare acknowledgment that conceptual knowledge is not a copy of reality, merely an abstract formulation based on interpretive and selective perception. One such acknowledgment came in the form of Thomas Kuhn's book *The Structure of Scientific Revolutions*.[11] Kuhn showed that scientists' perception and theory-building are influenced by concepts and theories that they are exposed to and accept in the course of their training and professional life.

Scientists do their work and interpret their data within a particular paradigm, a particular set of assumptions or beliefs about the world, or some part of the world. Kuhn showed that scientists don't operate in ways consistent with the assumption that science can give us knowledge of the world-as-it-is. Nevertheless, the assumption remains widely held. The insight that conceptual knowledge is not truth remains, for scientists as for educators, largely unacknowledged or soon disregarded.[12]

The mind is a tremendously valuable tool for building in the world of experience creations designed in the depths of Being.[13] And it is undoubtedly helpful sometimes, in limited contexts and practical matters, to label, define, categorize, analyze, evaluate and apply logic to elements of the world of form. "How do I propagate and cultivate this plant?" "How do I cook a tasty, nutritious meal?" On a larger scale... "How can we build a bridge?" "How do I program a computer?" This type of thought is the proper job of the mind.

It is wonderful to have a mind to investigate and answer such practical questions in life. It can give us conceptual knowledge that may have a certain provisional, instrumental value. But we don't know something just because we have named and defined it. Even our practical knowledge is not a copy of a reality supposedly existing objectively outside of us. A map is not the territory.

We tend not to see things freshly, as they are in reality, here and now. We don't usually meet a person or a tree or an object or a situation, not even ones we are familiar with: perhaps especially not the ones we are familiar with. *We meet our labels, assumptions and judgments about them.* And we have little or no awareness of who *we* truly are, caught up in an *idea* of who we are.

We tend to remain unaware that what we think we know — about the past, the future, what things mean, who we are and how things should be — exists only as imagination. We don't realize that it's just a conditioned operating pattern, just a provisional construction of the mind-body: ultimately not true, not real, just an illusion, just a dream. Then, we make the mistake of identifying the self with the fabricated operating pattern, with the dream. We allow the conditioned mind-body to take charge and the tail wags the dog.

Throughout your life, you have been constructing a complex web of beliefs, perceptions, emotions, memories, desires and behaviors. Your operating patterns have been conditioned by personal experience and exposure to the culture, especially at home, at school,[14] through the media and through ever-present advertising. You spent much of your childhood, in particular, imitating and playing games, practicing the game of life as you interpreted it and as you observed others playing it.

Most of this conditioning happened subconsciously, in the sense that you were so involved in it that you were not really noticing it. And it is in the nature of conditioning that you began to run on automatic most of the time. You became stuck in repetitive thoughts, memories, behaviors, experiences and emotions, which have been playing out, over and over, beyond your conscious control.

You became very attached to a lot of your conditioning. Your very sense of who you are has become tied up in it. The more attached you are to any particular thing, person, belief or concept of who you are, the more selective is your memory, the heavier is the mist distorting your perception, the stronger is your sense of separateness and the more troublesome are your emotions. You have interpreted many experiences in your life in such a way as to confirm and reinforce your conditioned view of yourself and the world.

Your conditioning has imposed a significance on reality which is not part of reality, but exists only as imagination, as what you think you know. Each individual's life is like a giant Rorschach inkblot test. Some psychologists use this test to help people to discover their perceptual filters, based on what they "see" in some inkblots. But your own life experience reveals the nature of your conditioned assumptions and values regarding yourself and the world. You create, manifest or attract the experiences you expect, whether wanted or unwanted. This is what some people refer to as karma.

Endnotes

1. These lines are from Wordsworth's *Ode: Intimations of Immortality from Recollections of Early Childhood* (Hutchinson 1964, p. 460).
2. See, for example, Heinz von Foerster's Principle of Undifferentiated Encoding (1981, p. 293).
3. For example, Dewey 1931; Hanson 1965; Kuhn 1962; Polanyi 1962.
4. Hanson 1965, pp. 5–19.
5. An Internet search on gestalt images will easily find the young woman or old woman image and other examples.
6. The clip comes from the DVD *Surprising Studies of Visual Awareness*, vol. 1 (2003).
7. Glasersfeld 1995, pp. 62–63.
8. Many investigators of learning and knowing have described this process of reconstruction of conceptual structures. Piaget referred to it as "accommodation" (1974, pp. 335–336).
9. Somchai struggled to make progress, was not greatly interested in his studies and knew that he was out of his depth. I don't know what became of him, as I left academia about a year later.
10. Kuhn 1970, p. 5.
11. Kuhn 1962.
12. In *The Psychology of Science*, Abraham Maslow describes the narrowly adaptive value of professional identities connected to the possession of particular bodies of abstract knowledge. He saw that intellectualism and science can be a defense, a way of avoiding life, and can serve a need for certainty, a need to be dominant and controlling, a need for "impressing

people often at the cost of part of the truth" and a need to be "satisfied with naming rather than experiencing... (a) common shortcoming of professional intellectuals" (1966, pp. 26–29, 33–39).

13. In his study of intuition, Tony Bastick concluded that "The famous intuitions and millions of other intuitions are responsible for every creation, device and man-made system of civilization to date. Some might say that it is our reason that has brought civilization this far, but reason is only the servant of our intuition" (1982, p. 2).

14. For example, William Pinar (2000) and many others have described how the very nature of the experience of schooling conditions us to see ourselves and others as objects and concepts, to doubt our internal signals and intuitions, to depend on external rewards and authority, and to comply with others' rules and expectations.

Chapter 3

The Life You Are Experiencing

(As you read on, notice that you are the awareness noticing that you are reading. When you think of it, come back to this: "I am the one noticing that I am reading." You could write this on a slip of paper to use as a bookmark. As you progress through the book, repeatedly place it a few pages ahead so it comes up as a reminder.)

Karma: How You Create Your Life

Humans function or behave in such a way as to maintain certain reference levels for a multitude of conditioned operating patterns felt to be important to the individual's survival and satisfaction. Perceptual Control Theory offers a testable model that shows that, actually, you don't consciously control or choose your behavior.[1] Rather, you automatically behave any way you must, so that what you perceive or experience matches what your conditioning says you should perceive. You control your perception, not your behavior.

Similarly, experiments conducted by Benjamin Libet showed that voluntary acts begin with unconscious processes in the brain, well before a person has a conscious sense that they want to act.[2] In a split second, you identify with the impulse to act that has already arisen spontaneously, and you have the illusion that you chose it. But your action has been prompted by your conditioned operating patterns.

More recent research in neuroscience and psychopharmacology has clarified some of the mechanisms involved in the determination of your perception and behavior. In her investigations into the "molecules of emotion," Candice Pert, for example, confirmed that, when we perceive stimuli in a new situation, our operating patterns created by previous experience affect our interpretation of and response to those stimuli.[3]

When you experience anything—a word, event, environment or personal interaction, for example—a whole set of biochemical processes is triggered within every cell of your body, changing the cells' functioning in many ways that correspond with previous states or responses. Memory is stored in biochemical receptors that are not just in your brain, but are on the outer surface of virtually every cell of your body. The perceptual history of each receptor affects how new information is processed, so that:

> the circuitry that will be chosen is a function of what came in the past. That's why... we have a tendency towards certain patterns, even things that aren't instincts. Everything we've learned in our whole life, all the emotional conditioning we've had, predisposes us, not just to certain thoughts, not just to certain movements, but even to specific ways that we hold our body: whether our shoulders are hunched in fear or whether they're standing back, proud and tall.[4]

You subconsciously function or behave to create or attract situations, experiences or states that will confirm a belief or fulfill a certain desired or expected emotional state and satisfy the corresponding biochemical craving of the cells of your body.

The Self-Fulfilling Prophecy

Robert Merton referred to this creative mechanism of human functioning as the "self-fulfilling prophecy," arguing that it is basic to the social sciences.[5] He observed how a belief or expectation, whether seemingly correct or not, affects the way people behave and the outcome of a situation.

As an example, Merton describes how assuming a situation to be real caused a thriving bank to fail. In 1932, customers of the Last National Bank, having heard and believed a rumor that the bank was heading for insolvency, lined up to withdraw their deposits. Until those customers held that belief, the bank was actually prospering. Once they believed the bank was foundering, they brought that reality about.

Robert Rosenthal and Reed Lawson conducted two interesting studies on the self-fulfilling prophecy involving rats. As a professor of social psychology at Harvard University, Rosenthal issued normal rats for each of his students to train to run in a maze (a Skinner box). He told half his students that they had been given rats that had been specially bred for poor maze performance, and the other half of the students were told their rats had been specially bred for good maze performance. In both experiments, the rats believed by their trainers to be better learners and maze performers performed better.[6] These studies suggest that the mechanisms of creating the experience we expect, of manifesting what we believe, are both subtle and powerful.

Rosenthal teamed up with Lenore Jacobson to explore this phenomenon further in a famous study involving the teachers and students of 18 classes of primary school students, from grades one to six.[7] They randomly selected about 20 percent of the students from each class. They gave their names to the teachers, telling them that a test of academic "blooming" showed that these students would show dramatic intellectual growth in the academic year ahead. After one semester, one year and two years, student IQ was re-tested. The students randomly labeled "intellectual bloomers" showed significant IQ gains compared with students in the control group.

The well-known and well-documented "placebo effect" is another illustration of the power of human consciousness to create physical realities of experience, when there is an unquestioned belief. Put simply, sick people get better when they fully believe something has been done to make them better, even though nothing has been done.

Bruce Lipton describes two examples of research

demonstrating the power of the placebo effect.[8] First, Dr Bruce Moseley, a surgeon at the Baylor School of Medicine, conducted a study of patients receiving surgery for severe knee pain. For one group of patients, Moseley shaved the damaged cartilage in the knee. For a second group, he flushed out of the knee joint material thought to be causing the inflammation. A third group received a mock surgery, including sedation, incisions and surgery talk, but no actual surgical procedure. All three groups received the same post-operative care, including a program of exercise. The placebo group improved just as much as the other two groups.

In the second example, Lipton describes the research of Irving Kirsch, based on data gathered in 2001 from the US Food and Drug Administration under the Freedom of Information Act. Kirsch found that the placebo effect could account for 80 percent of the effect of top anti-depressants in clinical trials. In more than half the clinical trials for anti-depressants, sugar pill placebos performed just as well as the drugs.

Your Vibes Affect You and Your Surroundings

Most of us think of the material universe as made up of solid matter, something concrete, static and predictable. We think of matter as having a molecular structure composed of the smallest units of material existence, atoms. But sub-atomic physics showed us long ago that this view is grossly inadequate. Within the atom are various sub-atomic particles, which take up a tiny amount of space compared with the total volume of the atom. Material objects that we like to think of as so substantial are actually almost completely made up of empty space.

This might seem curious but of little consequence since, nevertheless, atoms function and combine in such a way as to give us the seeming solidity and predictability of the material world. But could it be that we experience the world as a solid given, because we believe it to be so? Quantum physics tells us a lot more about what goes on at the sub-atomic level that has profound implications for how we see our role in relation to the life that we experience.

Atoms are made up of energy, not matter. Everything in our world is vibration. Sub-atomic particles are popping into and out of existence all the time. They exist in what is called a "super position," a wave or cloud of many possible positions. When it is not being observed, a "particle" is in all these positions at once. The instant we attend to it, it becomes a particle in just one of those possible locations.

The world is creative at this foundational level, since every time we observe, there is a new beginning.[9] No longer does it make sense to think of the world as being "out there," independent of us. Not only is perception an activity of constructing meaning, rather than merely a registering of the world-as-it-is. Quantum physics tells us that each of us *influences* the world that we perceive and experience.

Japanese scientist Masaru Emoto photographed ice crystals through a powerful microscope and discovered that different water formed different crystals.[10] He and his assistant found that water exposed to the vibrations of classical music resulted in well-formed crystals with distinctive characteristics. Violent heavy-metal music, however, resulted in fragmented and malformed crystals.

Emoto then wrote words on pieces of paper and wrapped the paper around bottles of water. Water exposed to the vibrations of "Thank you" formed beautiful, hexagonal crystals, but water exposed to "Fool" resulted in malformed and fragmented ice crystals. Water exposed to the invitational, volitional "Let's do it" formed attractive well-formed crystals, while water exposed to the authoritarian "Do it!" barely formed any crystals at all.

Human thought affects the structure of water molecules. One profound message in Emoto's research is that the vibratory quality of your thoughts and emotions, your state of consciousness, influences your own body, other people's bodies and the world around you, since much of the natural world, including people, is mostly water. And everything is vibration.

Candice Pert gives some graphic examples. One concerns people with multiple personalities. Their eyeglass prescription and allergies can vary from one personality state to the other. "One personality will be near-sighted. One will be far-sighted. One will be allergic to cats. One will adore cats."[11] She offers a second dramatic example of the creative power of human consciousness, from the work of psychiatrist and hypnotherapist Milton Erickson. He gave several flat-chested women the hypnotic suggestion that their breasts would begin to grow. All grew breasts within two months.[12]

The Inevitability of Suffering

One of the reasons most people hold many of their beliefs, feelings and subconscious assumptions about themselves and the world so firmly is that they look for and find confirmation of them in their experience. Even scientists prefer experiments designed to confirm, rather than to contradict an idea.[13] The conceptual identity, the "idea of me," would rather be proven right (validated) than wrong (caused to lose part of itself and thus to suffer).

The stronger our attachment is to conditioned patterns of belief and experience, the more the conceptual identity needs things to make sense in terms of those patterns, and the more distorted is our perception of reality. The interpretive and selective nature of perception and the subtle mechanisms of the self-fulfilling prophecy tend to give us the experience of whatever we believe or expect. Experience seems to be proving our beliefs to be true, proving our expectations of life to be valid, whereas it is actually only *reflecting* them. Do any examples from your own experience begin to suggest themselves?

What we think we know about ourselves and about life exists only as imagination. It has no ultimate reality. Our resulting experience of life is really a dream. For that reason, sooner or later our life begins to feel unsatisfying, troubling or downright unbearable. We experience this as disturbing thoughts and emotions, stress, illness, frustration, general unhappiness and discontent, in short, as suffering.

Responses to such suffering vary from one person to another. Some people only realize after many fruitless tries, and many people never at all, that their suffering cannot be solved using the same patterns and assumptions learned in the past. Many people continue to chase the experiences, things and identities they want or expect in the world of form. They never realize, or never accept, that these things do not and cannot give them peace, only fleeting satisfactions at best.

Distracting Yourself from Thoughts

An almost universally tried approach to dealing with suffering is to block out troubling thoughts with diversions. When you are distracted from your tormenting thoughts, you are fine, so people fill their lives with diversions and addictions to help them escape their thoughts. Among the many activities commonly engaged in as diversions are television, Internet browsing, social media, shopping, sports, hobbies and, of course, work.

The use of more intense, mind-body altering activities to escape disturbing thoughts is epidemic: things such as legal and illegal drugs, and compulsive sexual activities. There are many well-documented and proverbial costs of addictive activities, but as solutions to the problem of troubling thoughts they have the same drawback as general diversions; sooner or later they are over, and thoughts flood in again. That is why many activities can become addictive. As solutions to suffering they are of such temporary help that you cannot get enough of them.

Stopping Thoughts

Another way that people commonly try to avoid their disturbing thoughts is by attempting to push them away or stop them. Some meditation and concentration techniques are aimed at achieving this stilling of the "monkey mind." But when you try to suppress a thought, you just make it more likely to arise.[14] It is easy to quickly discover for yourself that suppressing a thought doesn't work. Give yourself ten seconds right now, and try to not think about a yellow car. Ready? One, two... ten seconds. How did you go? Were you free of yellow car thoughts?

We have seen why this approach is not helpful. Your mental resistance to a thought or image only strengthens your belief in its reality. And what you believe is real, tends to become your experience, whether you want it or not. Using the mind to still the mind just creates more mental activity, strain and frustration; and it perpetuates your pattern of experience.

Thinking Only Positive Thoughts

Something else that people very commonly try in order to avoid troubling thoughts is focusing on positive thoughts. In 1944, inspired by a sermon he had heard, Johnny Mercer wrote the lyrics to *Ac-cent-tchu-ate the Positive*, a song which became very popular because it suggests that this is the key to peace. Certainly, thinking positive thoughts feels better than thinking negative thoughts.

However, the thought that "I have a list of ten things I like about my life," for example, is just as problematic as its negative opposite, "I have a list of ten things I don't like about my life." The positive only exists in relation to its opposite. There is no good without bad. Focusing on positive thoughts is obviously better than focusing on negative ones. But if you like the idea that "There are ten good things about my life," then you will fear any person or event that threatens to change or take away any of those things. You will also fear any thought or opinion or experience that suggests that something else about your life is bad or not good enough.

Two central functions of the mind are its interpreting and assessing activities. We have seen that the conditioned mind is constantly making things mean something that is not part of reality. And a central part of what you make things mean is almost always a judgment about their relative goodness or badness. The conditioned mind frolics in a world of conceptual opposites.

Whenever you are buying into the conditioned mind's game of labeling things good and bad, you can't have one without the other; you can't prefer one without being fearful of the other. And that is the core recipe for suffering. Trying to mentally focus on the good or the positive is not the solution. It is the problem.

The Gift in Suffering

Are we all destined, then, to suffer throughout our lives, because of our alienation from the reality of the awareness Self? Must we spend a lifetime merely playing out our karma by unwittingly creating unsatisfying experience out of conditioned operating patterns? Not necessarily.

The key is to realize that it is not thoughts, as such, that take away your peace. It is not thoughts that draw your attention away from the awareness Self. It is your attachment to thoughts. It is *believing* your thoughts to be true. In particular, suffering is caused by believing your conditioned mind's judgments of good and bad to be true.

However, judgments of good and bad are not part of reality. They are *not* true. They are only points of view, opinions or stories that you tell yourself and others. William Shakespeare summed it up, when he had Hamlet declare that "there is nothing either good or bad, but thinking makes it so."[15]

Say I have a hammer and a screwdriver on my workbench. Which tool is better and which is worse? Neither is better or worse than the other. They are just different. If I want to put a screw in the wall to hang a picture, the screwdriver is a better fit for the job than the hammer. If I want to nail down a loose floorboard, the hammer will help me, but the screwdriver won't. However, good or bad, better or worse, are not part of either the screwdriver or the hammer.

Try this. Move one hand up and down a few times in front of you. Now move your hand side to side a few times. Which movement was better and which was worse? It doesn't make sense, does it? They were both just movements. Neither strikes you as better or worse than the other, because you are not associating either movement with any identity or outcome that you are attached to. Your mind is not overlaying a judgment on the factual movements.

Your conditioned mind is made up of beliefs about yourself, other people, things and experiences, which are basically judgments of good or bad, right or wrong, should or should not, valuable or worthless, supportive or threatening. Distracting yourself from the negative thoughts doesn't bring you peace for long, and trying to stop them or just focus on the good thoughts doesn't work either. How spiritually liberating it would be if you could look at your conditioned assumptions about your experience and discover for yourself that the judgment embedded in them is just an overlay on reality, that it is not true.

Giving your troubling thoughts, emotions and experiences *more* attention, rather than less, makes your conditioned patterns more conscious. The term "subconscious" simply refers to thoughts, operating patterns or habits that you have not usually been noticing. Many of the subconscious thoughts and operating patterns that determine your behaviors, emotions and experiences are actually familiar to the conscious mind. It's just that their operation is usually automatic and unnoticed.

Perhaps one of the reasons that the notion of having a "subconscious mind" has become so popular is that it diverts attention away from having to notice, question and deal with the thoughts and operating patterns that we are emotionally attached to, that we think are part of who we are. The problem with conditioned thoughts and patterns is not that we are completely unaware of their existence or their nature. It's that we have not been shown the benefits and methods of noticing them and questioning their truth.

The motivation to do this comes from your suffering and from the ultimately irresistible call of your awareness Self to come back to who you really are. Suffering is a wonderful invitation to question and unlearn old assumptions and patterns that you would otherwise have wanted to leave alone. Whatever form it takes, suffering can be a catalyst for spiritual awakening, the proverbial blessing in disguise.

Endnotes

1. Powers 1973; 1998.
2. Libet 1985.
3. Pert 1997; 2000.
4. Pert 2000, Disc 3, Part 6.
5. Merton 1968, pp. 475–476.
6. Rosenthal and Lawson 1964.
7. Rosenthal and Jacobson 1968.
8. Lipton 2005, pp. 139–141.
9. Goswami 1995, p. 42.
10. Emoto 2004.
11. Pert 2000, Disc 1, Part 11.
12. Pert 1997, p. 147.
13. See, for example, Klayman and Ha 1987.
14. Researchers who have studied this phenomenon refer to it as "ironic rebound." See, for example, Wegner 1989.
15. This is from Shakespeare's play *The Tragedy of Hamlet, Prince of Denmark*, Act 2, Scene 2 (Wells and Taylor 2005, p. 694).

Chapter 4

Questioning Conditioned Assumptions

(As you read on, notice from time to time that you are the awareness noticing that you are reading.)

The peace of formless awareness is your real nature, beyond the realm of your mind-body. However, conditioned operating patterns have constantly been making things mean something that they don't mean in reality, and you have had a habit of identifying with those meanings. You have been trusting them, because you have been assuming they were true. Conditioned thoughts focused on assessing yourself and the world around you—on judging them good or bad, right or wrong, enough or not enough—have constantly been drawing your attention away from your awareness Self, so that you have forgotten who you truly are.

When you break the habit of identifying with what is *not* you, you are left with what *is* you, the observing awareness beyond your mind. When you see through what the conditioned mind-body thinks things mean, in particular its judgments of good and bad, you awaken to your true nature as peace and oneness with the spiritual essence of all life.

Beliefs Can't Be Proven, Only Disproven

We have noted that people, including scientists, tend to look for and to find confirmation that their assumptions about the world and themselves are true. However, while experience seems to be proving your thoughts, assumptions and expectations to be true and valid, it is really only *reflecting* them. You cannot prove any mind-made knowledge to be true. You can only prove it to be false. In fact, the history of philosophy, both modern and ancient, Western and Eastern, is replete with this recognition that certainty about conceptual ideas is not possible. There are so many who have deeply investigated human nature and knowing, who have urged us not to hold *any* beliefs, either academic or everyday. Rather, they have urged us to suspend judgment and remain skeptical of all conceptual ideas, since they are only the mind's abstract constructions of reality that can easily be refuted.

Observing many instances which support an idea does not prove it. It does not guarantee that you will not see that idea contradicted in the future. That makes sense, doesn't it? Let's consider a very simple example. Alice may be observed, three days in a row, enjoying eating a mango. However, this does not prove an idea that "Alice enjoys eating mangoes." On the fourth day, Alice might be sick of mangoes. Or she might have a stomach ache and not be able to bear the sight of a mango. Or she might be very sad that her cat died unexpectedly and mangoes seem irrelevant. So an idea that seemed to be proven by observations on the first three days, ended up being disproven by an observation on the fourth day.

Instead of looking for or accepting confirmatory evidence of your conditioned beliefs, judgments and expectations, it is much more helpful for your peace and spiritual awakening to see if there is any contradictory evidence. *Just one observation at variance with an idea will prove that idea to be false.* Writing about whether science can give us true knowledge, philosopher of science Sir Karl Popper referred to this as a principle of falsification.[1] Of course, it also applies in ordinary life. "Alice enjoyed eating a mango three days in a row" is a fact. "Alice enjoys eating mangoes" is a belief, and it was proven to be false by just one observation.

Let us look at how you can use the principle of falsification as a simple but powerful tool in the service of your spiritual awakening. Huge benefits will flow from identifying your thought patterns and discovering that you actually don't know for certain that they are true. When you allow yourself to see thoughts and emotions for what they are, merely opinions of the mind-body that you can never prove to be true, you will release yourself from their hold. You will crack wide open the karmic prison, which is merely your conditioned assumptions. What remains will be the peace of the awareness Self.

Disbelieving Thoughts of Good and Bad

Imagine there is a busker on the street where you are walking, and he is singing and playing the guitar. There is nobody else nearby. There is an open guitar case in front of the busker, with a few coins in it. The singing is very ordinary, and you don't feel like throwing any money into the case. You walk past and the busker says to you, a bit despondently, "You are a total loser." What would you feel? Nothing much, probably. The busker doesn't know anything about you, and it's pretty obvious that he is just miffed that you didn't give him any money.

Now imagine that your spouse, or perhaps one of your parents, looks at you one day and says in a serious tone, "You are a total loser." What would you feel? You would probably feel defensive, hurt, perhaps even crushed. Why the difference in your reaction? You heard the same words from each person. The difference is because you didn't believe the busker's words, but you believed the loved one's words, at least to the extent that they triggered thoughts of self-doubt. So it was not the words or thoughts themselves that affected you. Believing or not believing the words is what made the difference.

Here, then, you have a simple and powerful key to freedom. You can never prove that a thought is true, but even one observation at variance with a thought will prove it to be false. Any time you think something is bad, ask yourself if you can think of any way in which it could be seen as good or could result in something good. You always can, so the thought that it is bad must remain unproven forever: not a true thought.

Note that this is not about thinking positive. It's not about convincing yourself that something that you thought was bad is actually good. No. It is about seeing that you cannot know for sure that anything is either good or bad, better or worse, as it should be or not as it should be. It is about suspending judgment. The examples I offer below, emphasize disproving thoughts that something is bad, but that is only because it is usually such thoughts that trouble people. You can't know for sure that anything is good, either. Let us look at just one example of that, before we look at a few thoughts that people often find troubling.

Imagine you are playing the poker machines, and you win the jackpot. You jump up and down with excitement. "I won! I won!" Do you know for sure that it's good that you won the jackpot? Is it possible that it could turn out to have some bad consequences? Perhaps the high of winning will cause you to become addicted to gambling, with a whole lot of unwanted consequences that often follow such an addiction. Perhaps you will get mugged and injured outside as you are leaving by some people who saw you win the jackpot. You have no way of knowing for sure that the thought that "It's good that I won the jackpot" is true.

Misfortune

You might think, "It's bad that I lost my job. Poor me! I'm so depressed." Is it misfortune to lose your job, or is misfortune merely a concept, a judgment, that the mind has overlaid on the fact of losing your job? Do you know for certain that your thought that it is bad that you lost your job is true? Could the opposite be true? Is it possible to think of some way in which losing your job is good or may lead to something good? You have no way of knowing what might flow from the experience of losing your job. You might get to spend more time with your spouse and children. You might get a job next week that pays more and you enjoy more. Your next job may give you valuable experiences that you would never have had otherwise.

Isn't it liberating to see that you can't know for sure that any event that happens or fails to happen in your life is bad? It is always possible to imagine some way in which what you thought of as misfortune might turn out to be good fortune. You cannot know. That is freedom. That is peace.

In the early 1990s, my then-wife had a couple of miscarriages. We thought these were bad events, and we felt very upset. Ten or so years later, we were both busy doing things with our lives, like combining work and study, moving and spending time away from home, that we probably wouldn't have been doing if we had children. I remember we looked at each other one day and agreed, "Isn't it good that we ended up not having kids together?" Another 15 years later, as I write, it seems even more fitting that I didn't have children.

Can you think of something that has happened in your life that you were not very happy about at the time, but which led in some way to a good outcome? As soon as you realize that you don't know for certain that something is bad, that the opposite could just as easily turn out to be true, or be thought to be true, the wind drops out of the sails of that thought. You are free of it and free of the troubling emotion it triggered.

This does not only apply to major events in your life. It applies equally to the many little things that happen or fail to happen throughout each day. Any time you are troubled by an emotion, even a minor one such as annoyance or disappointment, first acknowledge the emotion. Don't deny it or suppress it, but allow yourself to feel it. Then, notice that you are the awareness that is noticing the emotion. Shift from thinking, "I am frustrated," for example, to saying to yourself, "I am the one noticing a feeling of frustration." This will immediately put a little space between you and the emotion and assist you in disidentifying from it.

Then, look to see what thought is underlying the emotion.

What thought is triggering it? It might be a thought that you were barely aware of till you started looking. You may have been looking at what happened or did not happen as being the cause of your emotion. But remember, it is not a person, situation or event itself that triggers your negative emotions. Negative emotions are triggered by believing a thought that says the person, situation or event is bad.[2]

Anxiety

Let us say you are feeling a bit irritable. You snap a couple of times at your spouse or your child, and you realize that you are feeling a bit on edge. As you look at it, you realize that you are feeling anxious or fearful. Ask yourself, "What is the thought underlying my anxiety?" Then you remember that you have an interview at your bank tomorrow, to find out how much they are willing to loan you to buy a house.

You recognize that there is a thought that "It would be bad if they won't loan us enough to buy the lovely house we found last week." Then, question the thought. "Do I know that is true? Do I know that it would be bad for my life if we can't buy that house? Is it possible it could be good for my life?"

Then your responses come. "Well, yes. Perhaps I wouldn't have enjoyed that house. Perhaps one of the neighbor's children would have bullied my children. It's in the next town, and if we bought that house, I'd have a long commute to work each day. My children don't want to change schools and leave their friends. Perhaps next week we will find a less expensive house that suits us much better, a house that is closer to work and my children's school, a house that doesn't put so much financial pressure on us, or a house that has a deck and a garden for the children to play in. That is possible. I can't know all the flow-on effects of getting or not getting the home loan tomorrow. I cannot know, for sure, whether it would be good or bad for my life if we can't buy that house."

When you realize that you don't know for certain that it would be bad for your life if the bank won't loan you enough money for the house, the anxiety disappears. What remains? A feeling of peace.

Grief

You may feel a little shocked as you begin to realize that things that are accepted in our culture as legitimate reasons to feel bad are actually myths. They are not reasons to feel bad. Feeling bad is just a conditioned reaction, just a thought that you and many others have believed.

In the past, you may have believed things like, "My dog died! It's not only understandable that I'm grief-stricken, it's proper!" In fact, in 2001, I had this experience. As I carried my old and dying dog, Oscar, into the veterinary surgery to be humanely put down, I wore sunglasses. It was night-time. And yet, is grief proper? Is it necessary?

What thought underlies grief? Something like, "It's bad that such-and-such died," or "It's bad for my life that such-and-such died." Then come the deep sadness, the tears, the anger, the anguish. In such a case, allow the emotion to be there. Acknowledge it, without overly indulging it. Then consider if you know for certain that it's bad that the dog, or whoever, died?

First, you can ask yourself, "Is it inherently bad?" No. We have seen that nothing is good or bad in reality, only in thought. Remember the hammer and screwdriver? Just tools. The hand movements you made? Just hand movements. There is nothing good or bad, but thinking makes it so.

Second, ask yourself, "Do I know for certain that it's bad for my life that such-and-such died? Could the opposite be true? Can I imagine something good that might come out of it?" There would be lots of possibilities. You might learn to become more emotionally independent and discover a wonderful new freedom in your life. You might find another dog who greatly enriches your life in different ways than the one who died. You might decide not to get another dog, and that gives you more freedom to do new things that enrich your life.

You soon see that there is no way that you can know for certain that all the consequences of the death are bad ones. When you really see that there is actually no way that you can know that it's bad that such-and-such died, the grief lifts. Yes, the tender feelings are there, but the dark, overshadowing emotion is not. Does that mean you are heartless or uncaring? Not at all. It means you are present with what is, rather than caught up in conditioned reactions. And being emotionally unshaken makes you far better able to assist others who may also have experienced that loss.

An additional way to see that it is thoughts rather than the facts that are triggering grief is to imagine a scenario in which you volunteer the loss. Imagine, for example, that your adult sister visits from the other side of the country. She really hits it off with your dog. Your sister lives alone, and you decide to give her your little dog as a companion. She takes the dog home and you never see it again. Three years later, the dog dies of old age. Are you grief-stricken? Probably not. You are no longer having or believing a thought that "It's bad for my life that the dog died." Same fact, different thought.

Heartbreak

A similar process of questioning thoughts can be applied to other experiences of loss too, including the heartbreak and grief that people often assume is a necessary result of relationship breakups and divorce. In the above discussion of loss through death, we noted an additional aspect of conditioned beliefs that is very common. Most of our beliefs are held by many other people too. So, in questioning your thoughts that things are bad, you will often find yourself questioning ideas that are accepted as true by people close to you and by many in the wider culture.

Be willing to question common assumptions and conventional reactions to experiences, because they are just myths, just collective conditioning. If hundreds of millions of people believe an idea that is false, it's still false. Actually, many of the myths of modern culture are myths in two distinct senses. They are myths, because they can't be shown to be true, and the principle of falsification can quickly show them to be false. And they are myths in the sense that they are not as universally accepted as is commonly assumed. The notion of culture as consisting of a large group of people who all believe the same thoughts is itself a myth, the myth of mass culture.

Leading up to and following divorce or relationship breakups, a variety of troubling thoughts and turbulent emotions are very common. I struggled with many myself, when I felt the need to walk out of a 30-year marriage. Let us look at just a few of the thoughts that are common in connection with relationship breakups.

"An ended relationship is a failed relationship," which is to say that "It's bad if they end." Where is it written that relationships should last forever? Okay, it *is* written in some places, but they are called fairy tales. And for many people those fairy tales were powerful childhood programming. If you question these thoughts in the way shown in the previous examples, you will soon discover that you can't know for certain that it's bad that your relationship has ended. You will see that it is just as possible that good things will come out of it.

"There is something wrong with me or the other person if a relationship ends." Do relationships end because there is something wrong with one person or the other, or could it be due to either or both of the people realizing that their interests, values or beliefs are no longer a good match? Could it be due to either one or both people realizing that the other person can't make them happy, perhaps even that *no* other person can make them happy or complete them?

"It's not normal to be single after a certain age. It's normal to have a romantic or marriage partner." Who says it's not normal to be single, apart from fairy tales, traditional or modern? Are there not many single people of all ages? Are you able to think of any reasons why the thought that "It's bad to be single" is not true? Can you think of any advantages to being single? You will quickly think of some. Are you able to think of any reasons why the thought that "It's good to be married" is not true? Most married people will quickly offer you some!

"I need a man/woman to complete me and make me happy." Would finding or keeping a man or a woman make you happy? How could it? Having a man or woman in your life, whoever they are, cannot prevent you from experiencing the emotional and other consequences of believing thoughts. And single or coupled, the conceptual identity can never feel content and complete, because it is made only of ideas. Its very nature is separateness and insufficiency. Having a man or woman in your life can't give you the peace that can only come from spiritual awakening. Good and bad are not part of singlehood or couplehood. These are only thoughts. They are myths.

Loyalty

A powerful belief that many people struggle with, when contemplating or adjusting to a relationship breakup, involves the concept of loyalty. I want to mention it specifically. It is a major reason that many people put off a change that they really want to make in their life. And it is a major emotional burden that many people carry after ending a relationship. It was a tough one for me personally. "How do I leave somebody I care about, knowing that she will hurt?" Eventually, a few years after our parting, I got it. We have seen the answer.

Nobody's emotional hurting is due to what they are experiencing. It is only due to thoughts they may have and believe *about* what they are experiencing. You can't hurt anybody.

You cannot hurt anybody. They may *feel* hurt, if they believe a thought that says, "What I'm experiencing is bad or wrong or means that I'm unlovable." None of us has control over what another person believes. Therefore, none of us has control over another person's emotions.

"Do I know for sure that it's bad that somebody else is suffering? Is it possible that their suffering may lead to something good?" It certainly is. And that's not in your hands. Suffering is ultimately a gift that life offers each of us, to invite us to question our conditioned assumptions and awaken to reality. Of course, you don't go around causing suffering, saying, "Here, this'll help you." Equally, however, it is not your responsibility, and ultimately not even your possibility, to rescue another from the consequences of believing their thoughts. Don't mistake the compassion you feel for a thought of loyalty or obligation. When being true to your inner knowing is uncomfortable for another, that's their life. Yours is yours.

Loneliness

One of the most commonly troubling emotions on the planet is loneliness. It is epidemic. Many people, including most lonely singles, believe that loneliness is caused by being alone. But are all people who live alone lonely? It would only take one person who is single and does not feel lonely to disprove that belief, and there are many of those. Are single people who are sometimes lonely, lonely all the time? No. Often, when they are doing something they enjoy or doing something with a lot of focus, they don't feel lonely, even though they are alone. So loneliness among singles can't be due to being alone. It occurs when a thought arises in the mind that says, "It's bad to be alone," or "Since I am alone, there must be something wrong with me," and the thought is believed.

Any single person who believes, as many do, that one advantage of marriage is that you will never be lonely, is mistaken. A very large proportion of people who report being lonely are married and living with their partner. Something else is going on.

We have seen how, during childhood, conditioning creates a thick blanket of forgetfulness over the awareness that is your essential Self. Your sense of who you are becomes completely dominated by your mind, body and emotions. The constructed sense of self, the idea of who you are, is not who you are, and this is the true source of the feeling of loneliness. If you feel lonely, it is only because you have forgotten who you are.

It's pretty tough out there, as an egoic, conceptual identity. There is a constant, underlying sense that something is missing. It is, after all, merely a constructed sense of self. It is only made of ideas that are believed, and we have seen that no ideas can be proven true. They can only be proven false. The set of conditioned operating patterns that you have come to think of as who you are is a house of cards.

The egoic self holds on tight. It is afraid that its lack of substance may be discovered. It is worried that criticisms leveled at it may be true. It is constantly seeking to build itself up, fortify its position, find validation and support, prove its worth, get what it wants and feel good about itself. One of the most preferred mechanisms of survival of the conditioned self is to try to add to itself, complete itself or fulfill itself through another person: to feel validated, to feel approved of and to feel that it is okay and lovable.

Such external validation can temporarily be deeply satisfying to the egoic identity. Eventually, however, whether in a relationship or not, the true Self inevitably senses the unreality and irrelevance of the egoic self and its trappings. Something deep within you calls, "Please, come home." The true cure for loneliness is to experience the awareness Self, which is the One Life, the formless consciousness within all life. This is the longed-for sense of connectedness, wholeness and okayness.

Your conditioned thoughts and emotions have been, by definition, habitual. Questioning and disbelieving a conditioned thought will usually free you from its hold immediately, dissolve any associated emotion and leave you feeling peaceful. That does not mean the operating pattern will never trouble you again. Many years of conditioning and attachment does not fall away overnight. When you challenge a conditioned pattern, you will likely have some experiences that will tempt you back into it. Don't be surprised or discouraged when the thought and emotion return. Go through the process of questioning the thought again. Each time you do this the pattern will weaken further until, before long, it crumbles.

Every act of questioning conditioned assumptions about life, every act of recognition of what is not true and not you, is a step closer to the full awakening of the real you. You have seen enough of the process of questioning thoughts for you to be able to use this powerful tool to question and disbelieve thoughts about your experience. Let us now turn our attention in the direction of questioning thoughts about your conceptual identity, your idea of who you are.

Endnotes

1. Popper 1963. Popper suggested it would be more helpful if scientists tried to disprove ideas rather than to prove them, since they can never be proven: "The old scientific ideal of *episteme* — of absolutely certain, demonstrable knowledge — has proved to be an idol" (1959, p. 280).
2. Youtube videos by Noah Elkrief are excellent aids to seeing through thoughts that trigger specific emotions.

Chapter 5

Questioning Your "Idea of Me"

(Notice from time to time that you are the one noticing that you are reading.)

Through your many and varied life experiences, you have constructed an image of who you are: a conceptual identity, an "idea of me," "my story." It may contain, for example, ideas such as, "I am a devoted wife and mother. I'm a social worker and a tennis coach. I am American. I am confident with my friends, but I get anxious in big groups. I think I am very good looking, but I'm not very smart. I doubt myself a lot of the time, at least I think I do. I'm very loving and spiritual, and I hate shellfish and materialistic people." (I have tried to introduce a little humor here. If I have not succeeded, I'm okay with that. I'm not attached to a self-image of "funny person.")

Aspirational Self-Image

Identified as it is with the world of form, the mind-made sense of self easily gets drawn into trying to add to itself, complete itself or fulfill itself through form. We easily lose our awareness Self in admiring or wanting things. We lose ourselves by identifying with things, by making them part of our idea of who we are. The ego thinks that "If I *have* something special, or I am *associated* with something special, then I *am* something special."

There are all sorts of "good" things that an ego might love to add to itself: wealth; a special make of car; a lovely house in the "right" suburb; an attractive face or body; an attractive wife or husband; a family; a university degree; a skill or talent; a profession, business or trade with status or distinctiveness; a champion sports team, music idol or movie star; name-brand clothing; membership of a special club, culture or nationality; and on it goes. There is no problem with any of these things in themselves. But when we create from them an idea of who we are, we lose consciousness of our awareness Self.

As I write, a few days ago millions of Australians celebrated Australia Day. No problem. There is nothing wrong with liking Australia. I like living in Australia too. It would, however, cause considerable loss of spiritual awareness, if I believed that "Australian" is who I am. "Australian" is a concept. It is not who I am. If I went to live in Canada, for example, I would not cease to be me. (I'd be an Australian, living in Canada. LOL.)

Here is a similar example of adding to the self-image by identifying with a place and a sports team. Years ago, I was talking with an estate agent, looking for a small piece of rural land to create a hobby farm. The agent said that he had just what I was looking for, within the distance that I had specified.

"But," he added, "you wouldn't be interested in that piece of land."

"Why wouldn't I be?" I asked.

He said, "It's just over the border, into New South Wales (the adjoining state)."

"Why would that be a problem?" I asked.

Surprised at my continued interest, he explained, "Most of my clients would never consider a piece of land in New South Wales. They would no longer be 'a Queenslander' and couldn't barrack for the Maroons (the Queensland Rugby League football team) against the Blues (the New South Wales team)."

For many people, "Queenslander" and "Maroons supporter" are *who they are*. "Go the mighty Maroons!"

Are there some items in the above list of things egos often like to identify with that you noticed apply to you? Or perhaps there is something not on the list? It could be a car, for example. Follow me, with one of your items in mind. Consider two statements: "I drive a BMW" and "I am a BMW driver." There is a subtle, but significant difference. The first is a mere statement of fact. The second has a different structure and tone that implies identification. "I am..."

Can you make two similar sentences for your item? Can you feel a difference between the two statements? Next, using your statement that reflects some identification, say to yourself, "I am the awareness noticing the thought that 'I am a BMW driver' (or whatever your item is)." You are not the thought, but the one who is *noticing* the thought. This introduces a bit of distance between the awareness Self and the thought, between Self and BMW. It begins a process of disidentification.

It will help you very much in awakening the awareness Self if you take some time to make a list of all the things you identify with, that you think are part of who you are, and with each one, go through the simple exercise I just described. You could use as prompts the list I wrote above of "good" things that egos often like and the sample self-image I described at the start of this chapter. Of course, doing this exercise does not mean that these things should go from your life, or that you should stop enjoying them. But it will free you tremendously to see that they are not actually who you are; they are part of your experience, but not part of you.

Defeatist Self-Image

The "idea of me" is the most powerful set of beliefs that operates, through the subtle mechanisms outlined in Chapter 3, to create your experience of life. But self-image is complex. The ego's efforts to build a strong conceptual identity will not necessarily focus on identification with things in the world of form that some groups and cultures regard as good or special. Very often, even more limiting ideas of being an underdog, rebel, victim or battler also form a large part of the "idea of me." The self-image of "Aussie battler," for example, is a prominent part of Australia's cultural ethos.

Some years ago, I watched a current affairs television program, which was a follow-up to a program about young adults who were long-term unemployed. Following the first program, the owner of a tropical island resort on Australia's Great Barrier Reef contacted the producers of the program to say that he may be able to offer a job to some of the people featured. The producers of the show contacted some of the unemployed people to tell them about the offer of jobs, and the follow-up program that I watched reported on what happened.

One young man was flown to the resort for an interview. Everything looked promising. However, the applicant had very long hair, and the resort owner explained that he would need to have it cut, since neat, short hair was the standard in such high-class international resorts. The applicant refused to cut his hair and passed up the job offer.

Long hair, and some associated anti-establishment attitudes of the young man, were so much a part of his idea of who he was, that he was unwilling to cut his hair. The consequence that he quite consciously accepted was that he still had no job. Of course, it may well be that having no job was itself a part of this young man's self-image. I don't mean to imply any judgment here, though there was a pretty clearly implied judgment in the television program. I simply offer it as an illustration of how the "idea of me" influences experience.

Am I Good or Am I Bad?

The realm of mind is a world of conceptual complexities and opposites. Your mind interprets the world by perceiving and choosing between differences. Its two core functions are interpreting and judging. The culture you grew up in is also dominated by mind, and of course you learned very early that, more often than not, it is better to be good than bad, right than wrong, confident than insecure, brave than frightened, clever than stupid and on and on.

Your "idea of me," consisting as it does only of ideas, is in a constant state of uncertainty and tension between opposites. Your conceptual identity is nowhere near as black and white as you might tell yourself or others. The ego will very often change its idea of who you are.

With regard to nearly every idea you have about yourself you have, in the past, had thoughts, comments from others and experiences that contradict it. For example, imagine that, when you were a child, some other children teased you one day after you got an answer wrong in class. They circled around you in the playground, mocking you: "Stu-pid. Stu-pid. Stu-pid." You felt really... well... stupid. You went home and told your mother, and she said, "Don't worry, Darling. They are just bullies. You aren't stupid." But something of both ideas would linger in your idea of who you are.

The mind-made identity is a complex of often contradictory ideas. Consequently, many people often feel a sense of uneasiness, inadequacy or guilt lurking in the shadows of the mind.

I Choose the Good! Can I Do That?

From time to time, everybody is troubled by a self-image thought that contradicts some other aspect of their self-image. For some people this is rather frequent, and for others it is an almost constant self-talk of criticism and defense.

A frequently suggested antidote to this tension is the use of positive affirmations. These are statements you might regularly tell yourself, or perhaps have stuck on the fridge or bathroom mirror, which affirm the opposite of the troubling thought. "I'm not good enough," "There is something wrong with me" and "I'm unworthy" are common troubling thoughts. Accordingly, perhaps the most commonly recommended and used affirmations are ones like, "I love myself," "I approve of myself" and "I am a good and lovable person."

However, since positive only exists in relation to negative, positive affirmations ultimately tend to make the problem worse. It may make you feel better for a short time to read an affirmation that says, "I approve of myself." But your mind knows very well that sometimes you don't approve of yourself, and it knows that yesterday, or ten years ago, you did or said something that you feel bad about. That's why you are saying the affirmation!

Focusing on positive thoughts obviously feels better than focusing on negative ones. However, positive affirmations ultimately heighten your fear of any thought or opinion or experience that might suggest the negative opposite. You can't have the good without the bad. Positive affirmations also strengthen your idea of who you are, which is not who you are.

Since there is no good without bad, if you want to think of yourself as a good person, there is no option but to compare yourself with others, or with situations, and find ways to perceive them as bad, wrong or inferior. Egos attached to a self-image of "good person" (and which ego is not) tend to do a lot of criticizing, rejecting, complaining, blaming and making others wrong or inferior.

Here is an everyday example. Much of Australia is very dry. In rural parts of the country, a common conversation when two blokes meet in the street goes something like this.

"Geez, we could do with some rain!"

"Yep! Bloody dry!"

What has happened? Two egos have strengthened themselves by making themselves right and good, and the weather wrong and bad. Let us look at another illustration.

You might try to sustain a self-image of "good person" by showing obvious indignation at receiving bad service when shopping. If that was a strong pattern within your conditioned self, you would certainly create or draw to yourself many opportunities to display annoyance about receiving bad service. The egoic self would also savor the feeling that "I deserve better" in your memories of those experiences and, especially, as you related the story to others.

You may not be so quick to acknowledge your part. You may not be aware that you actually created for yourself most of those experiences of bad service by the energy you had been putting out, by your expectation of and your need to perceive bad service. It's just like a magnet, invisibly pulling and pushing particular energies and polarities around it.

You might "forgive" the shop assistant who spoke to you abruptly or served you mechanically or kept you waiting unnecessarily in the store yesterday. But the very act of forgiveness would be, in that instance, a way of strengthening the egoic identity. The egoic mind would be thinking, "I let this person off the hook, despite the fact that they were in the wrong and I was in the right." And you would continue to attract similar experiences, until your emotional attachment to that kind of experience and ego pay-off was dissolved.

Do I Know for Sure That I'm Bad?

Your conceptual identity may often be troubled by an emotion that has been triggered by a judgmental thought about itself. The thought may arise internally or it may be triggered by criticism from outside. If this is sometimes your experience, remember that you cannot ever prove an idea to be true, but you may be able to prove it to be false. Rather than running from the judgmental thought to some positive thought, acknowledge the negative thought. Face it head-on and allow it to be there. Then question it, so that you can discover that you don't actually know for sure that it is true. In this way, rather than strengthening your conceptual identity, you gradually dismantle it.

Am I Really Stupid?

Let us take the earlier example, "I am stupid." Apply the principle of falsification. "Can I think of an experience in which the opposite was the case?" Sure, so stupid can't be who I am.

"Could somebody else think I'm not stupid?" Yes, there are multiple people who have told me I am clever, so stupid can't be who I am. "Is stupid part of reality or is it a concept of the mind?" Ah, yes, it's only a thought. Stupid and smart aren't part of me or anything that I do, aren't part of reality. "Who is aware of the thought about being stupid?" Ah, yes, I am the awareness Self noticing my thought, so I can't be the thought. The feeling of inadequacy has dissolved.

But I Feel So Guilty

What about feelings of guilt? "I feel guilty for speaking unkindly to my sister last week," or "I feel guilty for cutting off that car in the traffic today." The emotion of guilt arises when you believe a thought that "What I did was bad" or that "I am bad, because of what I did."

Ask yourself, "Are good and bad part of what actually took place or are they concepts in the mind?" Ah, phew! The actual act was neither good nor bad. Next, ask yourself, "Do I know for certain that all the consequences of my action will be bad for the other person?" Well, you have no way of knowing all the effects of your action, do you? Even if the other person expressed criticism or anger at your words or actions, neither they nor you can know if all the effects will be bad. "Is it possible that the other person could experience some good effects from my actions?" Sure, that's certainly possible.

Finally, ask yourself, "Am I to blame for what happened?" We have seen that, until you are spiritually awake, you don't actually choose your actions. Your behavior is just an inseparable part of conditioned operating patterns. You are not your thoughts or the actions associated with your thoughts. You are the awareness that notices thoughts and actions as they come and go. You don't choose the thoughts that pop into your head. We have noted some of the great lengths that people go to in order to avoid their thoughts. Why would people bother, if they are able to simply choose whatever thoughts they want? If you chose your thoughts, you would never choose ones that create conflict or bad feelings. You would only choose thoughts that make you feel good, or maybe no thoughts at all.

Summing up, then, what you said or did was in itself neither good nor bad. There is no way to know for sure that all the consequences for the other person will be bad. And you didn't actually choose to say those words to your sister or to cut that car off. The feeling of guilt is suddenly gone.

You Lousy #$&*!

We will briefly consider one more troublesome emotion, and that is anger. As we noted earlier in this chapter, egos attached to a self-image of "good person" tend to do a lot of criticizing and making others wrong. In some egos, this need to feel superior is so strong that there is actually an attachment to anger. "Angry person" can even be, for some people, a part of their self-image. Whether or not this has been the case for you, let us here assume it is an unwanted emotion.

"I'm angry at such-and-such, because of what he or she said or did to me." This situation has similarities to guilt, except that this time the shoe is on the other foot. You ask questions about what another person did, rather than about what you did.

"Was what the other person said or did factually bad or is bad a concept I have overlaid on reality?" Nothing is good or bad, in itself. "Do I know for sure that what the other person said or did to me will have only bad consequences for my life?" No, I can't possibly know what all the flow-on effects will be. "Can I think of any possible good consequence that could come out of what they said or did?" Perhaps it made you more aware of the effect on others of your own words and actions. Perhaps what was said or done to you upset you so much that you began to question and discover what really causes your negative emotions. Finally, "Is the other person to blame for what they said or did?" No, it flowed inevitably out of their conditioned operating patterns. They didn't choose their thoughts, words or actions.

Beyond Forgiveness

This brings us to a lovely serendipity: releasing the hook that is hidden in the judging mind's concept of forgiveness. Earlier in this chapter, I gave an example of how the act of forgiveness can be a way of strengthening the egoic identity: "I will overlook what you said or did, despite the fact that you were in the wrong and I was in the right." We tend to think of forgiveness as such a noble and applaudable act. But just as you can't have good without bad, you can't have forgiveness without assumptions of wrongdoing, guilt and blame.

You can't consider forgiving another without first believing that they are bad or that they did something wrong. And you can't hope for self-forgiveness or another's forgiveness without first believing that you are bad or have done something wrong. The concept of forgiveness strengthens the conditioned mind's identity and love of judging. More profound than forgiveness is disidentification from the judging, conditioned mind. This peacemaking is the true Self's recognition that *there is no bad or wrong to be forgiven.*

If you feel bad about something you have done in the past, you truly make peace with yourself when you realize that it wasn't bad at all, in reality, and it was not your true Self who did it anyway. This true resolution of bad feelings comes as you recognize that there is nothing to forgive. There is no wrongdoing, no guilt and no blame, because any judgment has been seen to be untrue, just a figment of imagination.

Similarly, if you disapprove of or feel angry about what another person has done in the past, you truly make your peace with them when you realize that it wasn't bad at all, in reality, and it was not their true Self who did it anyway. And one step further. If you feel angry or disillusioned over what life has brought you or has denied you, you truly make peace with life when you realize that it was a gift to help you to wake up out of the illusion of the judging mind to what is real. Nothing has ever been bad; only thoughts have said it was so.

Thoughts Don't Mean Anything About You

It is a wonderfully liberating thing to realize, not only that you cannot know that thoughts are true, but also that thoughts are not you. You are the awareness that notices thoughts as they come and go. Thoughts just arise by themselves, mostly due to your background of experiences, your programming. They aren't important. They don't mean anything about you. Thoughts do not mean anything about you.

You can't know for sure that thoughts are true, and you don't choose them. When you remind yourself of these two facts, you are disidentifying from thoughts and conditioned operating patterns. You are opening to the awareness Self that notices perceptions, thoughts, emotions, actions and experiences. Remind yourself frequently throughout each day that "The thoughts that pop into my mind aren't reality, aren't true. They are just thoughts," and "I am the one noticing thoughts and perceptions. I'm not the one thinking." Each time you disidentify from thought in this way, you will immediately feel more peaceful. Not only that, but you will also progressively weaken the habit of identifying with conditioned patterns of the mind-body.

As identification with the mind-body weakens, you can allow thoughts and emotions to come and go as they do. They won't take away your peace, because you no longer believe them or mistake them for who you are. In fact, the coming and going of thoughts, emotions and actions gives you another opportunity to notice that you are the formless noticer of your life in the world of form. You can just *be* there, noticing and enjoying the peace of the here and now.

Chapter 6

Seeing What Is Real

I hope that you have discovered for yourself that the mind is not the reliable faculty you were taught to believe. The primary functions of the mind are twofold. First, it loves to construct abstract interpretations. Second, it loves to see differences and to judge them. When you identify with these processes, the awareness Self gets forgotten, and the ability to see reality is lost.

However, we have seen that what the mind thinks it knows can never be shown to be true, though it may easily be shown to be false. This amazing insight frees you to more easily experience the reality of life. Now, let us look at several ways of experiencing or noticing what is real, that are particularly helpful to spiritual awakening.

Noticing Your Experience

The first approach to noticing involves your immediate experience and circumstances. It consists of noticing your present moment experience, *as it is*, instead of noticing and believing judgments about it.

As you disbelieve and disidentify from thoughts more and more, you will naturally find it easier to allow your experience to be whatever it might be in any moment. After all, it is only thoughts that tell you that what you are experiencing is bad or wrong or not good enough. Most people have these kinds of thoughts, either intruding intermittently or nagging virtually all the time as a kind of haunting self-talk. But now, you have discovered that such thoughts are fictions. They are not part of reality, merely judgments overlaid on what is.

Your experience in the world will always be limited in some way. And nothing stays the same for very long. That is the nature of the world of form. However, your conditioned mind's resistance to these limitations and changes, its judgment that "The way things are right now is not good enough," or that "What has happened is bad," keeps you trapped in thoughts, negative emotions and clouded perception.

You may not always recognize your resistance to your present experience as being resistance. You might more often notice it as looking forward with hope to the future, or perhaps as looking back with nostalgia on your past. But looking to the next moment for a satisfying outcome, or to the past for a sense of who you are, is a rejection of what is. It takes you away from the awareness Self and reality, into imagination.

Naturally, it is necessary from time to time to draw on information from the past and to make plans for the future. That's no problem, so long as it doesn't involve a rejection of your present experience. We have seen that getting what you want, and therefore the future in general, can't bring you peace and fulfillment. Only questioning thoughts and experiencing the awareness Self beyond thoughts can bring you peace. Forgetting this and looking away from the here and now to something better in the future fills the present moment with thoughts and feelings of insufficiency.

Note that this noticing of your experience without resistance is not about mentally agreeing to put up with a situation or event, despite not being happy about it. Remember in the previous chapter, we saw how the concept of forgiveness holds some judgment within it; it only exists in relation to assumptions of wrongdoing. In a similar way, words like acceptance can have connotations of being willing to put up with something, despite not wanting it to be that way. When you hear the encouragement to accept that things are as they are, you might easily respond by thinking, "Okay, I'm willing to accept the situation, even though I don't really like it." This "acceptance" by the conditioned mind is a begrudging acceptance; like forgiveness, it still holds within it a disapproving judgment. It does not liberate you from the egoic mind, but keeps you identified with it.

The key to a liberating noticing of your present experience is to recognize that you do not and cannot know for sure that what you are experiencing is bad or should be different. This allowing of your experience to be as it is, is not an acceptance of something that is not the way you would want it to be. It is seeing through and giving up any judgment that your experience is either good or bad. It is seeing that you don't know for certain how things should or shouldn't be.

Does noticing your present experience without judgment mean you should not respond to it and perhaps make changes? Not at all. Sometimes you may feel it is not possible or appropriate or necessary to change the situation, and just allowing your experience to be as it is enables you to feel at peace with it. But often you may feel it is also entirely appropriate to respond to the situation. Noticing your experience without judgment simply means that you no longer shut down the awareness Self by rejecting or resisting what is, feeling or saying to yourself that "This shouldn't have happened," or "She shouldn't have said that," or "Things shouldn't be this way." The reality is that it *did* happen, she *did* say it and things *are* this way.

There is a gift inherent in allowing the reality of what is. Architect Frank Lloyd Wright saw this and observed that "Limitations seem to have always been the best friend of architecture."[1] Allowing that the way things are right now is the way they are, leaves you feeling peaceful and present, even as you may speak or act to deal with or respond to what is. And in this case your speaking and acting draw intuitively and creatively on Universal Intelligence, since your awareness Self beyond thought is the formless organizing principle that flows through all life.

This attitude of conscious allowing, then, is a very simple and very effective way of becoming spiritually awake. Now, you could set aside some time to regularly practice this "allowing what is," if that appeals to you. You could do a sit-down version of this practice of being in the here and now without judging it, to make it into a "meditation practice." But a strong word of caution. You don't want to become attached to a specific, structured practice as your way into being the noticing awareness.

It won't really help your awakening if you peacefully "allow the moment" just during occasional 20-minute windows of time. That is a deception: really, rather meaningless. It can easily result in feeling that "I can accept the moment without any problem. It's my life that I don't like!" In that "training the mind" approach, both "the practice" and "the moment" have really become abstractions, separated out from the events of your experience.

Noticing your present experience without judgment brings you into the awareness Self, because the allowing without judgment is a putting aside of the egoic mind. In order to have the peace of spiritual awareness, you want "noticing what I am experiencing without judgment" to be a new way of being. All the time. Make it a practice to frequently remind yourself throughout each day that you allow your experience to be just as it is in that moment. Whatever form your experience is taking you notice with full awareness, without judging it, without wishing it was different. This is being spiritually awake.

As I have said, this includes allowing that whatever thoughts have arisen in your mind have arisen in your mind. Don't resist them by thinking that "I shouldn't have thoughts like that," or "I don't want thoughts like that." Thoughts happen. You don't choose them.

Let thoughts come if they come. The natural mind can notice any kind of thought without suppressing or resisting it and without indulging or following it. It remains merely a thought. There is no belief, attachment or identification, as there is with the conditioned mind. As you continue disbelieving and disidentifying from thoughts, you will increasingly find that you can allow any thought that arises without trying to push it away or distract yourself from it. Simply remind yourself that "I am the awareness noticing this thought that has popped up." If a thought that another thought is bad, wrong or unacceptable nags at you, question whether you can know for certain that this added judging thought is true.

Noticing the Energy of Your Inner Life

You have been disbelieving thoughts about the past, the future, what things mean, who you are and how things should be. As you withdraw consciousness from the mind in this way, it is naturally left with itself, with the inner life. As you have been doing this, you may have occasionally noticed a pleasant and subtle energy in and around parts of your body, such as your hands.

Perhaps you have previously had this sensation from time to time. This is the energy of your inner life, your true Self. You have tended to identify with your physical body and with thoughts, but you are more truly this subtle life energy in and around the body. It is your subtle, yet tangible connection with the formless Universal Life. It is easy and most beneficial to feel this energy of your essential reality.

If you don't feel this subtle energy at all at present, continue to practice all of what I speak about in this book. Here is something else you can do. First, in order to stop all your attention flowing outwards into your mind and surroundings, put your attention on your breath. Notice its natural movement in and out of your nostrils. Do this for half a minute or so. If thoughts pop up, that's fine. Remember to just notice them, without rejecting them or following them. They are not true and not you. Allow them. Then, let your attention again be on noticing the sensation of the movement of your breath.

Next, bring your attention to one of your hands. You will be less distracted by the physical sensation of touch if you position your hand comfortably a little away from the body and other objects. With your eyes closed, and keeping your hand still, notice your hand. You will probably begin to notice a subtle feeling of energy in and around your hand. If you do, open your eyes and notice that you can still sense that energy.

You didn't feel it before, only because your attention was drawn away into the physical world and the mind. Once you locate that subtle feeling, it's easy to be with it. That subtle life energy is the essence of the Life that you are. Notice that the feeling is so subtle that it cannot be truly referred to as a perception, in the usual sense, but a feeling of beingness. "I *am* that energy" feels to be more the case than that "I (subject) am *perceiving* energy (object)."

Now, notice the energy in your other hand. Can you feel some energy in your feet? Your legs? Your arms and chest? What about your lips? Now your face? Next, slowly scan your body from feet to head, feeling the inner energy as you go. Finally, spend a while, just as long as is comfortable, noticing the field of energy in and around your whole body, homing in on particular areas occasionally, as you feel to.

Noticing the life energy in your body is a lovely way of coming into the awareness that is your true Self. It is a beautifully peaceful and beneficial practice to just sit for a while, noticing the energy of your inner life. When the conditioned mind tries to reclaim your attention with a thought, that's fine. Allow it. It's just a thought: not true and not you. Notice that you are the one noticing the thought. Then, withdraw attention from the mind again, noticing the energy.

This is something you can do pretty much at any time, the more frequently the better. You can do it in bed, before sleeping and upon waking. You can do it during momentary breaks at work, while cooking dinner or while waiting at the traffic lights. Everything you do that doesn't require a lot of concentration, you can begin to do with your whole being, with some of your attention remaining on your inner energy.

Noticing Sensory Objects

The next approach to noticing involves giving receptive attention to sensory objects that are present with and around you. Noticing things more attentively and receptively both flows from and leads to being less identified with thoughts: with labels, categories, definitions and judgments. This is not a grasping or agenda-driven attention, but a soft and receptive noticing by the stillness of the awareness Self. Receptively noticing sensory objects allows you to experience them more as they are in reality, without making them mean something, without imposing a mind-made significance on them.

You can do this with nature, with people, with your own body and with man-made objects. Whatever it is, observe the thing as though you had never come across anything like it before. No preconceptions. Check in with all applicable senses. Notice the parts and the detail. Notice the whole. Notice, even, that the object is connected organically with other objects and events in space and time: that even the perception of the thing as a discrete and static object would be an artificial act of the mind. Avoid getting caught up in naming, categorizing and judging. Avoid admiring and fault finding. Of course, don't get annoyed with yourself when you inevitably do get caught up in these habitual processes. Just notice that this has happened. Then, put aside again, as best you can, your perceptual filters, and come back to passively observing with empty awareness.

Particularly with sensory objects in and from the natural world, you will find that this receptive noticing enables you to resonate with the subtler life of which those things are only the outer expression. A stone thrown into the turbulent, wind-whipped surface of a lake, quickly disappears without a trace. However, even a small pebble thrown into a glassy-still lake sets up a very clear pattern of ripples. In like fashion, with the usual turbulence of our labeling, analyzing and judging mind, we find it difficult to register much more than the superficial features of the world around us. Even then, we perceive them in a distorted, selective and influencing way. When you deliberately put aside preconceived notions and personal agendas, however, and you notice things in this attachment-free way, mental activity will recede and you will be better able to resonate with the inner, energetic qualities of natural objects and people around you.

When you make a point of noticing in this receptive way, you will find yourself feeling a deeper connection or oneness with the world around you. Botanist George Washington Carver who, being a freed slave, never had any formal schooling, expressed this simply and eloquently when he noted that "Anything will give up its secrets if you love it enough."[2] The kind of love which is "enough" is not the attachment-charged thought "I love you," but the love which is the very nature of your awareness Self beyond thought. From this unconditioned level of awareness, you will begin to sense the essence of things outside as being the same as the essence of who you are.[3] It will be most helpful to your awakening to notice things and people in this receptive way, wherever you are and whatever you happen to be doing.

Noticing the Noticer

As you become more used to allowing your experience to be just as it is in any moment, used to feeling the subtle and peaceful life energy in and around your body, and used to receptively noticing things around you, you are becoming the conscious noticer of life. It becomes easy to notice that you are the awareness Self noticing stillness, noticing perception, noticing thoughts coming and going, and noticing behavior happening.

During your daily activity, make it a frequent practice to look at something, while noticing that you are the one noticing the seeing. "I am the awareness noticing that I am seeing the table." "I am the one noticing that I am seeing my cat." Listen to things, any things—a bird, a piece of music, voices or traffic in the distance—without allowing all of your attention to flow outwards to the object of perception or to thoughts about it. "I am the one noticing that I'm hearing an ambulance siren. I am the awareness noticing the thought that perhaps someone has been in an accident."

When going for a walk, driving, eating, washing the dishes and engaging in other simple acts, notice that you are the awareness noticing these behaviors happening. "I am the uninvolved noticer of what is happening." You are not truly the one doing these things; you are the one noticing them being done.

Feel the subtle energy of your inner life, and notice that you are the one noticing that perception or activity is happening, or that thoughts are popping up and passing. This noticer is the real you that has always been in the background, largely asleep or veiled, behind the scenes of your life experience. Now it is coming to the fore as wakeful presence. As the awareness Self, you are becoming the conscious witness of your life. Consciousness is becoming conscious in you.

Endnotes

1. Wright 1954, p. 46.
2. Quoted in Buhner 2004, p. 155.
3. In his book *The Art of Loving*, renowned psychoanalyst Erich Fromm also saw this. He noted that, in the kind of love that transcends the prison of separateness and penetrates the secret of another's soul, "I know in the only way knowledge of that which is alive is possible for man—by experience of union—not by any knowledge our thought can give" (1995, pp. 23–24).

Chapter 7

Some Traps to Beware Of

(Notice from time to time that you are the one noticing that you are reading. That is spiritual awakening.)

As you progress with questioning your conditioned assumptions and old identity, and you begin to experience the arising of the awareness Self, the conceptual sense of self will begin to fall apart. It won't be all smooth sailing. There may be some bouts of fear, despair or grieving as you let go of aspects of a life and identity you have been attached to. There may be tears.

Don't be dismayed. Stay true to your real Self. See the sacrifice of old patterns of conditioning that you had mistakenly put your trust in as the very thing that is opening you to the incomparable peace and blessing of spiritual awakening. Be aware, though, that seeing its end in sight, the ego will try to find a way to survive. It will look for ways to strengthen itself by keeping you identified with the mind-body.

The Complexity Trap

Be wary of the false and unhelpful cultural assumptions of complexity around spirituality and awakening. Explored by the mind, the subject is endlessly complex. First, it is complex because no belief or conceptual statement can be proven true, but they can all be refuted. Second, it is complex when explored by the mind, because concepts can never grasp formless awareness.

Some years ago, I went to check out an informal self-discovery group that met once a month in someone's home in a nearby town. The hostess wheeled out a trolley with two shelves laden with books about personal growth and spirituality: perhaps 50 or more. I was shocked. I imagined that people who were a bit newer than I to inquiring into self-awareness would likely feel, "Oh my god! You mean it's that complicated?" No, it's not! It is simple and natural.

The formless consciousness that interpenetrates all life is who you are now, beyond the mind. Spiritual awakening is a structural change in consciousness. It is not about analyzing, fixing or adding to the complexities of the conditioned content of your mind-body. It's not about personal growth, self-improvement, spiritual development or similar abstract concepts that have no ultimate reality.

Don't give the job of spiritual awakening to your mind. You are not your mind. Spiritual awakening is about making a simple, structural change in consciousness by noticing that thoughts are not true and conditioned operating patterns are not who you are. It is about noticing that you are the awareness that notices thoughts, perceptions and actions as they come and go.

The "Spiritual Me" Trap

The ego does not mind what conceptual identity it has, so long as it has one. It is very good at shape-shifting. As your values change to prioritize spiritual awakening, what better strategy for the ego than to take on or strengthen an identity of "spiritual person"? It would be a huge win for the egoic self if it could allow you to believe you are on a path to spiritual awakening, while you are actually playing into the hands of the ego. How could the ego pull off such a trick? By allowing you to believe that liberation from the illusion of your identity with form can be achieved through form.

You sabotage your spiritual Self when you take on the conceptual identity of spiritual seeker. The more elaborate and rigid the teachings and practices (forms) that you become attached to as the means to a goal of finding the true Self, the more elusive the true Self remains.

Language can be a valuable tool, but more often it is a tyrant, wielding huge, delusionary power. Do you remember how in Chapter 2 we saw that the conditioned mind sees everything through a heavy mist of perceptual filters? In the gorilla story that I related, I was told to focus on "white" and "counting." Boom! I couldn't see a black gorilla that was there before my very eyes.

There are some seemingly harmless words in "spiritual" culture that have the same blinding effect. Consider terms like "spiritual seeker" and "spiritual journey." What do they both strongly imply? The future! Looking, looking, looking. Trudging, trudging, trudging. Where does the future exist? Only as imagination. It never comes. Like the pub with a sign out the front saying "Free Beer Tomorrow." By contrast, consider words like "noticer," "observer," "awareness" and "presence." The thought-based ego is happy enough for you to be on a path to an imagined future. It is not so comfortable with the fact that you can drop into the awareness Self in an instant, or with the fact that, from this awareness, you can easily notice the unreality of thoughts. Don't identify with being a spiritual seeker.

Don't become identified with elaborate "spiritual" disciplines or emotionally attached to the trappings of spiritual culture. The ego will be attracted to outward signs, pastimes, objects and places that have the appearance of being spiritual, because they will reinforce a conceptual identity of "spiritual me." There is no real problem with enjoying some of the trappings of spiritual culture for their own sake. But be very cautious. They are a minefield. Don't imagine that they will make you a more spiritual person. Any *idea* of who you are is the very thing you are wanting to see through, to dissolve, to empty out. Emotional attachment to anything that you think will lead you to who you are already is a trap.

Many millions of people, in both the East and the West, have spent a lifetime immersing themselves in elaborate "spiritual" techniques, rituals and culture that come out of ancient traditions, in the belief that these things will bring them peace. How many of these people have experienced spiritual peace and awakening? Only a handful. Is this not a handful of coincidences and many millions of instances that disprove the belief? A false idea that's very old is still a false idea.

The appeal of cultivating so-called spiritual thoughts and spiritual feelings can also be a trap. Does it matter, from the perspective of the awareness Self, whether the thoughts that come and go are negative or positive, profane or "spiritual"? You are not the thoughts. Whether subdued and mundane or elevated and "spiritual," you are not your moods. All these are merely forms that are noticed by the formless awareness that is you, the true Self.

Devotional affectation and excessive displays of gratitude for or dependence on a teacher or guru are another big trap. The Self is not external. *You* are the Self. There is nowhere to go, nothing to become, nothing to be given. There is no need for devotion or dependence. Don't sell yourself short. Don't sell the Self short. You have it all. It's just that you have been believing a thought that you don't. There is a humorous cautionary tale about a student of Zen, who saw an old, awakened master on the opposite side of a wide, swiftly flowing river. The student waved his arms wildly and shouted, "Master, Master! How do I get to the other side?" The old man smiled and called back, "You are *on* the other side."

When you feel the draw and the tickles of awakening, which spell the beginning of the end for your illusory "idea of me," be alert to any attempt by the ego to hijack the awakening process by strengthening or shape-shifting to a "spiritual me" identity. In the movie *The Jackal*, Bruce Willis disguises himself as a policeman in order to carry out his function as an assassin. Like this, the conceptual identity will often disguise itself as a "policeman," looking after the interests of the inner you, when it is actually the "assassin," looking after its own interests.

The "Unworthy Me" Trap

As awakening progresses and threatens the ego, another trick it will play to strengthen itself is to make you feel unworthy of spiritual awakening. Of course, this may just be felt as an intensification of a lifelong tendency to self-doubt and criticism. Nearly everyone lives with at least a vague feeling of guilt or inadequacy, entrenched since their early years. It is the natural consequence of the universal desire of the conditioned mind to think of itself as good.

Now, the *concept* of spirituality is culturally intertwined with notions of good and bad. This is a huge myth and so ironic, since we have seen that goodness and badness, worthiness and unworthiness, and all the other conceptual opposites exist only in the realm of mind, whereas spiritual consciousness is beyond the realm of mind. The conditioned mind's judgments of good and bad have nothing whatever to do with the true Self, which is the formless essence of you and all life. However, pretending that they do enables the ego to entice you back into identification with concepts and judgments. The "unworthy me" identity is a very sneaky and ever-present trap.

We have seen that we don't choose thoughts. They just pop into the mind: all and every kind of thought! Judgmental thoughts, selfish thoughts, sexual thoughts, arrogant thoughts and all the rest: they just happen. Be careful not to indulge or follow thoughts based in attachment, if you can help it. Question them. Disidentify from them. But don't feel shame for their arising. The part of the ego that wants to be good and spiritual strongly resists so-called bad thoughts, which causes them to persist. They may well intensify and play out in word and action. Another part of the ego feels glad to feel bad, because its identity has been strengthened.

When feelings of guilt or shame arise over supposedly unspiritual thoughts, see those feelings for what they are, just attempts by the conceptual self to add substance to itself. The ego is thinking, "If I can't be a spiritual person, at least I can be an unworthy person. Then I exist." Berating yourself will just strengthen the illusion that the egoic identity is you.

Instead, when self-condemning thoughts arise in response to other thoughts, acknowledge and even verbalize that "This is the conceptual identity trying to add substance to itself." Thoughts and emotions like, "I'm guilty," "I'm unworthy," "I'm not spiritual enough," "There is something wrong with me," "I feel ashamed": these are very appealing refuges for an ego on the run. See them for what they are: signs of an ego trying to strengthen an "unworthy me" identity.

Don't be tempted to believe self-condemning thoughts. In the way shown in Chapter 5, question whether you know for certain that they are true. You will find that you don't. Also, are you not the awareness Self noticing those thoughts? So you can't be the thoughts. Everything bad that you have ever believed about yourself is false. It was just the judging play of the conditioned mind, just a figment of imagination.

Dissolving karma through spiritual awakening has nothing to do with accumulating enough good karma. It has nothing to do with being good enough or spiritual enough to deserve awakening. And it has nothing to do with being offered the opportunity to awaken or find peace, despite your being bad or unworthy. We often hear the word "grace" used in connection with spirituality. Grace is another word that can be a great trap.

The dictionary definition of grace is "courteous goodwill." In connection with spirituality, the concept of grace implies the somewhat undeserved intervention of an imagined divine being or an embodied enlightened being bestowing blessings on you, guiding your life or making you good or more spiritual. Hundreds of millions of people are right now caught in the "unworthy me" trap, buying the conditioned mind's story that they are an undeserving wretch. They are passing up the opportunity to leave their karmic prison and awaken to their true nature as the awareness Self by questioning their conceptual identity. Instead, they are strengthening their egoic self by identifying with a teacher, guru, guide or external power, who they believe has overlooked their supposed unworthiness and bestowed his or her grace upon them. This is what happens in religious conversions, and it is also common in "new" spirituality. Can you see what a disempowering trap this is?

Grace, if there be such a thing, is built into your essential nature. It is in the very nature of consciousness to want to become conscious. Don't adopt the identity of disciple or devotee or follower or sinner, or defer to some supposedly higher authority or being, whether in this world or some other. Appreciating inspiration or encouragement is one thing, but you don't need a minder, go-between or redeemer. You are the Self.

The "Imperfect Me" Trap

Don't obsess over so-called bad habits that you may have. What you or others may call bad habits are conditioning. They are not you. If you have some habits that you feel are based in neediness and ego gratification, and are ultimately not in harmony with the true Self, don't indulge them more than you have to. But don't beat yourself up over them either. That will just strengthen the egoic identity.

Practice being the noticing awareness Self, and you will find that attachments will weaken more and more, and associated behaviors will fall away. If and when the true Self wants some behavior to stop, it is more than capable of making it clear that the behaviour is driven by the ego and of dissolving attachment enough to make stopping possible. In such cases of inner knowing, you will have received guidance from the true Self, rather than judgment of and from the conceptual identity. There is an important difference. It may seem ironic, but you need to let go of the mind's self-judgment, before you can let go of the attachment-driven behavior. Don't let the conditioned mind turn it into an issue of good and bad, which have no reality. Don't fall into the trap of forming or consolidating a conceptual identity of "imperfect me" by overthinking things.

When an impulse arises to engage in some habit that you would rather not have, notice that you are the awareness Self noticing the desire or impulse. You are not the conditioned desire itself. If you find that you still give in to the behavior, be the observing awareness while engaging in it. Allow the fact that you are engaging in that activity, without judging yourself for it. Notice that you are the one noticing the activity taking place. This will assist in dissolving your identification with the behavior and your attachment to it. It will create a space between you and the behavior that gradually opens up the ability to choose.

The "Clever Me" Trap

Of course, your so-called good habits and achievements are also merely conditioning. They are not you. Don't be proud of them. That will just strengthen the conceptual identity. There is a lot of talk these days about how important it is to find your passion. But when you are full of passion, the One Self can't get a word in edgeways. Let go of your passion. Let go of needing to make a difference. The Universe has it sorted. You might still engage in an activity that you enjoy and have a talent for, but let go of your emotional attachment to it. Let go of your mind-made sense that your passion is who you are or adds something good to who you are.

There is a story of the Buddha which, while perhaps not historical, is nevertheless illustrative.

A follower asked the Buddha, "Master, are you a god?"

"No," replied the Buddha, "I'm not a god."

"Are you a celestial being?" continued the follower.

"No, I'm not a celestial being."

"Are you a human being?"

"No, I'm not a human being."

Perplexed, the follower asked, "Then, what are you?"

"I am awake."

Only when you let go of agendas and a conceptual identity can the Universal Intelligence move through you, as you. Don't think of yourself as anything. Become comfortable with being empty.

When you are empty, you can allow things, people and situations to come and go as the One Life needs them to, without resisting, grasping or interfering. Empty, you can be at ease with the flow of life in the world of form and change, realizing that it is the flow of Being, the play of the One Self. Empty and receptive, you can shine into the world as a unique expression of the formless organizing principle. This is truly being yourself.

Whether you are a health food fanatic or a junk food addict, a pauper or a millionaire, an illiterate or a professor, a celebrity or a prison inmate, you are not to blame or to credit for it. It means nothing about you. It is only a reflection of your conditioning and your experiences, which aren't you. You are not your story. Like the blank cinema screen behind the projected movie images, you are the witness of the story of your life.

The more often you drop into the awareness Self, the more support and direction you will receive from the One Self to dissolve conditioning and to experience and express the Universal Intelligence that you are. As awakening progresses and the noticing awareness comes in more and more, less of what you do and say will be determined by conditioning. But you are still not the one saying or doing things, except inasmuch as you are now one with the formless awareness that is Life. Can the "idea of me" take any credit? Be empty. It is the One Self working through you, dancing you. It's not your personal merit.

The "Must Get It Right" Trap

As you practice being the noticing Self, you will find from time to time that a peaceful intuition arises. In general, you will more and more often sense that a situation, decision or action is either true for you or not true for you. Following such intuitions will not be a case of mentally choosing between notions of good and bad or right and wrong, but rather of following what seems most deeply real for you, rather than what somehow seems to be less real. As you disidentify from conditioned patterns, you will increasingly sense that these knowings come from a deeper place than your mind's old, conditioned concepts and rules of good and bad.

But don't become obsessed with trying to work out in your mind if your every word and action comes from your real Self or from conditioned patterns. As you are awakening out of the conceptual identity into the awareness Self, looking for the source of your motivations and actions can feel like you are in a hall of mirrors. Don't become frozen by self-doubt, mental debating and second-guessing. "Does the Universal Self want me to do this or that?" "I feel like doing such-and-such, but I don't know if it's coming from my true Self or the ego?" "I was just talking with someone, but I don't know if everything I said came from my true Self."

Don't overthink your actions! It's okay for you to be you, as you are now. Allow that you are as you are now, and live from there. If what needs to be said or done next seems clear to you and comes with a feeling of calm, then follow that. Any time a decision or action is required, but the appropriate course does not seem clear, consider your true values and the likely consequences of each option, as best you can. Drop into the awareness Self for a while, then make your decision.

The great thing about the Intelligent Universe is that everything is set up to bring you eventually home to the One Self. Nothing that is ultimately real can be lost, missed out on or threatened. But in all your apparent choosing and doing, just notice that you are the awareness Self noticing it happening.

Chapter 8

A Few Tips and a Simple Strategy

(Notice that you are the one noticing that you are reading.)

You have read this far. If you still resonate with the formless treasure to which my words have so cumbersomely pointed, then I salute you. As I have said, spiritual awakening is about you making a simple, structural change in consciousness. You are breaking a habit: a big one, but just a habit. Up to a point, the mind's need for a viable structure of understanding had to be satisfied. I have sought to paint a picture, in broad strokes, to assist you with this.

Now, having discovered and recognized a structure of understanding that hopefully "makes sense of it all," you don't want to get further entangled in the mind. From here on, the formula for spiritual awakening is simple:

Disbelieving Thoughts + Being the Noticer = Spiritual Awakening

Is this enough, all that I have written? Yes. Sort of. Almost.

Limit Your Exposure to Unconsciousness

We have seen how the egoic identity will play all kinds of tricks to try to keep you identified with the mind, identified with ideas about your life and who you are. But the mind-based world, also, is full of seduction—pitfalls, dead ends and boggy ground—most of it purporting to be healthy, fulfilling or spiritual. As you question the truth of thoughts with your left hand, the world will try to pull you back into emotional attachment to form by your right hand, so to speak. A certain amount of strategy will pay dividends for you.

Look for ways in which you can minimize your involvement in

the wild storm of mental, emotional and behavioral conditioning in the surrounding culture. Take steps to shield yourself from the bombardment of conditioned input, such as through television, technological superficiality, spending unnecessary time around spiritually unconscious people and the like. These will easily take you out of the awareness Self and seduce you, in so many subtle ways, into identification with and attachment to form. The culture can seduce you into again believing that having some external thing, situation, experience or identity is necessary for your fulfillment.

Schedule some time frequently with your phone, Internet and email turned off. Television turned off. Music turned off. Can you schedule half an hour of alone time each day? An hour? And an afternoon a week? A day a month? More?

Try to spend some of that time with nature. The elements of nature and its overall grandeur and mystery speak to your essence. Formless consciousness within nature resonates with formless consciousness that you are. It calls that subtle awareness forth and helps to free you from the illusion of your identification with form. Nature is always accessible to you. It is enough if it can only be the tree outside your window or the clouds passing across the sky or a fresh flower in a glass of water on the table.

Simplify Your Life

What is most important to you? What do you truly stand for? Use your new clarity about your values, or your primary value (awakening and expressing the true Self, if such is the case), to make all your decisions about where you put your attention, time, energy and money. Where might you begin to put less of those things? You may find it very helpful to declutter your life.

Consider what is not serving you any longer and whether you might release it from your life. Go through your home, for example, each room, each cupboard, and consider selling, donating to charity or throwing away the things that you don't need or that aren't "you" anymore. Clear out clothes that you don't wear or that no longer feel right when you wear them.

Don't rush your decluttering or make any change in your life on an impulse. Consider what you feel you don't need anymore, then give it some time. If the feeling to let some things go remains in your times of calm and presence, then you might go ahead and let them go.

This activity can clear away a lot of stagnant energy of attachment to form. It can leave you feeling lighter, fresher and more spiritually awake. This is a good exercise to do once a year. Each time you declutter, you will shed more things that have been subtly binding you to old attachments and "ideas of me." You may increasingly see that you can live a peace-filled, spiritually conscious life without getting or keeping all that your conditioning and culture have been telling you is needed to be happy. You will find that living simply and appreciating the little things in life becomes not only possible, but very satisfying and supportive of your awakening.

Free Up Your Mind with Humor

Another great way to clear out stuck energy is to enjoy some humor. It's so easy to take spiritual awakening, and life in general, way too seriously. Humor is a gift to humanity. It helps you to break up the rigidity of the conditioned mind.

The great value and appeal of humor is that, when two previously isolated contexts or ideas collide in a joke, the result is a sense of being liberated from the prison of your judgment-laden, habitual ways of seeing things. Any time you realize that you are taking things very seriously, introduce a little light humor. Since humor loosens the grip of the mind, a few jokes about even unrelated subjects will help to liberate you from an overly serious mood. Enjoying a bit of humor regularly is also a great preventive.

Shall we do a little of that now?

Two men are drinking in a bar. After quite a few drinks, one man looks at the other and says, "I think I should tell you I've been sleeping with your mother." The second man pauses, looks the first steadily in the eyes and says, "Go home, Dad, you're drunk."

Another:

Two old men are drinking in a bar. One says to the other, "If I die first, I want you to pour a big bottle of beer on my grave every year on my birthday." The other says, "Do you mind if I filter it through my kidneys first?"

Bar jokes not appropriate in a book about spiritual awakening? Is that part of the facts or a judgment about the facts? Remember not to get caught up in conceptual notions of what is spiritual and what is not, or in a fictional identity of "spiritual person." Perhaps bar jokes aren't your cup of tea? Boom-boom. What about this one, about staying healthy and living long?

Walking is a great form of exercise. My mother started walking five miles a day when she was 60. Now she's 97, and we don't know where she is.

Or this one?

I almost had a psychic girlfriend once, but she left me before we met.

Or this one?

Two mind readers meet in the street. One says, "Hi, you're fine, how am I?"

One more.

A man takes his Rottweiler to the vet and says, "My dog has gone cross-eyed. Is there anything you can do for him?"

"Well," says the vet, "let's have a look at him." So he picks the dog up and examines his eyes. Then he listens to the dog's breathing, and he looks to see if his nose is wet or dry. Finally, the vet says, "I'm going to have to put him down."

"What, because he's cross-eyed?"

"No, because he's really heavy."

Okay, last one!

Before you criticize someone, you should walk a mile in their shoes. That way, when you criticize them, you're a mile away, and you've got their shoes.

In humor, two or more different perspectives run into each other and clash. Their assumed truth or rightness is shattered, and the tension in each is released in laughter. Humor subverts the authority of your ideas. You see them for what they are, merely conditioned inventions of the mind. Hence, the proverbially therapeutic effect of laughter.

A Simple Strategy for Spiritual Awakening

When you finish reading this book, you don't want to put it on your bookshelf and just carry on with your life. Do you? And you don't want to just make a mental note of a few practices and intermittently go to them as the emotional ups and downs of life come and go. These are certainly options, and there is no problem with these responses, if they seem right for you. But for you to get the most benefit from this book, I recommend two things.

First, I suggest that you use this book as a practical manual during your awakening. You may have read quite quickly to this point. The mind is naturally voracious, being curious about what interesting new bit of information may lie ahead. But when you finish the book, I suggest that you read it again very soon, at least a second time and preferably many more, taking it more slowly and especially taking time with all the practical and experiential aspects. You may be surprised at how the gradually clearing mist of your mind enables you to discover and experience more with each reading.

Taking notes or underlining sentences or sections that really speak to you will help you to take it in more deeply. You could also put some of your favorite bits in memos on your phone for easy reference and inspiration wherever you go. Immerse yourself thoroughly in the book, so that the energy of this very different mode of being really seeps into your bones. After doing that, read different parts of the book from time to time as you feel any clarification or inspiration might be helpful.

My second suggestion is that you use a simple piece of scaffolding that I will describe next, to help you to apply in your life the insights and practices I have discussed. It will also help you to stay on track for the long term. Without such a piece of scaffolding your old automatic pilot will take you along the old paths. The inertia and resilience of the old ways are very substantial.

I have described four general practices to incorporate in your daily life, or I would rather say to incorporate in your *way of being in your daily life*. Each of these approaches to living will be found to be effective in awakening the awareness Self. First, disbelieve thoughts by questioning whether you know for certain that they are true. Notice that you are not your thoughts, but the awareness noticing thoughts as they come and go. Second, notice your present moment experience without judging or resisting it. The mind doesn't know how things should or shouldn't be. Third, withdraw consciousness from the mind by noticing the subtle life energy in and around your body. As you engage in perception and activity, don't allow all of your attention to flow out, but keep some attention on the energy of your inner life. Fourth, receptively notice sensory objects, without imposing a significance on them. Also notice that you are the one noticing what is happening.

Each of these simple practices on its own is very effective in bringing you back to the formless awareness that is the real you. Become familiar with practicing each one of these openings to the awareness Self. Then, greater benefit will be enjoyed by making all of them a part of the way you live. They are each closely related and really bridge one to another naturally and easily. You can carry a simple mental and physical signpost with you in your daily activity that will link these practices together to be deployed in any and every suitable moment.

This signpost is in the form of an acronym: DAWN. Dawn is what helps you wake up, right?

D: Disbelieve thoughts. "Do I know for sure that this thought is true?" "I am not my thoughts. I am the one noticing thoughts as they come and go."

A: Allow your present moment experience to be as it is, without judging it. "Nothing is wrong, in reality."

W: Withdraw attention from your mind by noticing the subtle energy in and around your body.

N: Notice sensory objects receptively, without preconceptions or agendas. Notice also that "I am the one noticing what is happening."

You can write this signpost to spiritual awakening on slips of paper or post-its, and put them where you will see them frequently, such as on the dashboard of your car, in your purse or wallet, on your computer or smartphone, on your fridge and so forth.

Some of these physical signposts might include all of the words given with the acronym above. Others might have just the first word that follows each letter (Disbelieve, Allow, Withdraw, Notice), and still others might simply have the acronym letters: DAWN. Either way, once you are familiar with what the letters stand for, you will find this simple signpost takes only seconds to reawaken your spiritual Self.

Consider adopting DAWN as your primary-value homing thought. Use it as an anchor or reference point to frequently hold in mind. Let DAWN be your new default perceptual filter or, rather, your perceptual filter remover. The frequent and continued interruption of conditioned thoughts and attachments will break the old operating patterns and clear the mist of spiritual sleep from your mind. DAWN will help you to be more consistent in being the noticing awareness Self than the conditioned mind is in distracting you from it.

As you set out to reclaim the formless Self, your consciousness is relatively saturated with attachments to form: concepts, things, people and so on. By questioning thoughts and dropping into the observing awareness, conditioned patterns will weaken and fade. They will cease to dominate your consciousness and your life experience, though they won't disappear altogether. You will always have a residue of the person you have become through your background of experiences.

Your consciousness will eventually become dominated by the peace of the awareness Self. The balancing scales of your awareness will tip from predominantly identification with form to the light of the awareness Self shining through as the subtler and primary reality.

The Future or the Present?
To feel the draw of spiritual awakening is inherent in your very nature. But don't become mentally preoccupied with how that will ultimately play out. When you wonder, "How long will it take for me to wake up completely?" consider this. Who is asking? It is not the awareness Self. Don't become attached to a future state of "enlightenment." That attachment is the conceptual identity, fond of the idea of adding something wonderful to itself. The essence of enlightenment is being in the mode of awareness beyond mind, being the noticer. You can drop into that noticing awareness in an instant with DAWN. That is being spiritually awake. Wondering about a future state will keep you identified with the mind.

Allow yourself to be led, to be lived by the One Self. Let go of trying to control your life. Let it unfold for you. Live as simply as seems practical and right for you. Allow yourself to be content dealing with the small things or with what is presenting itself to be attended to. Address any matters, large or small, that you have been avoiding, but which won't go away. Otherwise, be content being small, being undemanding, being empty.

As you awaken spiritually, your uniquely individual expression of qualities and talents will come to reflect a humble creativity that taps the spiritual power of Life. Your expression will arise not from mind, but from the One Self, so that it spontaneously respects and nurtures you, others and the world.

As you experience freedom from identification with form, you will awaken to the formless essence of you as peace, contentment and oneness with all life. People, things, events and thoughts will lose their power to trouble and manipulate you. You will experience the here and now as it is in reality: filled with a subtler and more profound truth and beauty than your mind is able to fathom. In the words of John Keats:

Thou, silent form, dost tease us out of thought
As doth eternity... (and to man thou) say'st,
'Beauty is truth, truth beauty,' — that is all
Ye know on earth, and all ye need to know.[1]

Endnote

1.   These lines are from Keats's *Ode on a Grecian Urn* (Barnard 1988, pp. 345–346).

About the Author

For more than four decades, Andrew Seaton delved deeply into educational philosophy and psychology; old wisdom and new science; reports of higher consciousness; and a wide range of personal development, holistic wellness and spiritual awareness practices. He has had lots of different jobs, but his working background was mostly in education. He had many different roles in that field, most of them relating to education of the whole person. Eventually, Andrew came to see that in our world we are generally making some deeply flawed assumptions about knowledge and human nature. In 2006, he resigned from a two-year stint in academia in order to focus on unlearning his education and other conditioning, and on awakening the fuller functioning that he had come to see so clearly is possible and desirable. His spiritual awakening began in earnest in September 2018. Andrew is now focused on sharing with adults his practical insights into spiritual awakening.

www.AwakeningMadeSimple.org

A Message from Andrew Seaton

Thank you for reading *Spiritual Awakening Made Simple*. I do hope that you find it a helpful and rewarding companion for your life and awakening. If you have enjoyed the book so far and you have a few moments, please feel free to make some comments about it at your favorite online site for reviews. This will help others to become aware of the book and to enjoy and benefit from it as you have. If you would like to stay connected with my offerings, I invite you to visit my website for news about my services and forthcoming talks and programs.

Kind regards,
Andrew Seaton

www.AwakeningMadeSimple.org

References

Barnard, J. (ed) (1988) *John Keats: The Complete Poems*, London, Penguin Books.

Bastick, T. (1982) *Intuition: How We Think and Act*, Chichester, John Wiley & Sons.

Black Elk (1988) *The Sacred Pipe: Black Elk's Account of the Seven Rites of the Oglala Sioux*, Brown, J. (rec and ed), Norman, University of Oklahoma Press.

Buhner, S. (2004) *The Secret Teachings of Plants: The Intelligence of the Heart in the Direct Perception of Nature*, Rochester, Bear & Company.

Descartes, R. (1996) "Second meditation" in Descartes, R. *Meditations on First Philosophy* (trans. J. Cottingham), Cambridge, Cambridge University Press. First published 1641.

Dewey, J. (1931) *Philosophy and Civilization*, New York, Putnam's Sons.

Emoto, M. (2004) *The Hidden Messages in Water* (trans. D. Thayne), Hillsboro, Beyond Words Publishing.

Foerster, H. von (1981) *Observing Systems*, Seaside, Intersystems Publications.

Fromm, E. (1995) *The Art of Loving*, London, Thorsons.

Fukuoka, M. (1978) *The One Straw Revolution: An Introduction to Natural Farming* (trans. C. Pearce, T. Kurosawa and L. Korn), Emmaus, Rodale Press.

Glasersfeld, E. von (1995) *Radical Constructivism: A Way of Knowing and Learning*, London, RoutledgeFalmer.

Goswami, A. (1995) *The Self-Aware Universe: How Consciousness Creates the Material World*, New York, Jeremy P. Tarcher/Putnam.

Hanson, N. (1965) *Patterns of Discovery: An Inquiry into the Conceptual Foundations of Science*, London, Cambridge

University Press.

Hart, T. (2003) *The Secret Spiritual World of Children,* Maui, Inner Ocean.

Hutchinson, T. (ed) (1964) *The Poetical Works of Wordsworth,* London, Oxford University Press.

Huxley, A. (2004) *The Perennial Philosophy,* New York, Perennial Classics.

Klayman, J. and Ha, Y. (1987) 'Confirmation, disconfirmation, and information in hypothesis testing', *Psychological Review,* vol. 94, no. 2, pp. 211–228.

Kuhn, T. (1962) *The Structure of Scientific Revolutions,* Chicago, University of Chicago Press.

Kuhn, T. (1970) "Logic of discovery or psychology of research" in Lakatos, I. and Musgrave, A. (eds) *Criticism and the Growth of Knowledge,* Cambridge, Cambridge University Press, pp. 1–23.

Libet, B. (1985) 'Unconscious cerebral initiative and the role of conscious will in voluntary action', *The Behavioral and Brain Sciences,* vol. 8, no. 4, pp. 529–566.

Lipton, B. (2005) *The Biology of Belief: Unleashing the Power of Consciousness, Matter and Miracles,* Santa Rosa, Mountain of Love/Elite Books.

Maslow, A. (1966) *The Psychology of Science: A Reconnaissance,* Chicago, Henry Regnery Company.

Merton, R. (1968) *Social Theory and Social Structure,* New York, The Free Press.

Pert, C. (1997) *Molecules of Emotion: The Science Behind Mind-Body Medicine,* New York, Scribner.

Pert, C. (2000) *Your Body is Your Subconscious Mind* (CD Set). Boulder, Sounds True.

Piaget, J. (1974) *The Grasp of Consciousness: Action and Concept in the Young Child* (trans. S. Wedgwood), London, Routledge & Kegan Paul.

Pinar, W. (2000) 'Sanity, madness, and the school', in Pinar, W.

(ed) *Curriculum Theorizing: The Reconceptualists,* Berkeley, McCutchan Publishing, pp. 359–383.

Polanyi, M. (1962) *Personal Knowledge: Towards a Post-Critical Philosophy,* Chicago, University of Chicago Press.

Popper, K. (1959) *The Logic of Scientific Discovery,* New York, Basic Books.

Popper, K. (1963) *Conjectures and Refutations: The Growth of Scientific Knowledge,* London, Routledge & Kegan Paul.

Powers, W. (1973) *Behavior: The Control of Perception,* Chicago, Aldine.

Powers, W. (1998) *Making Sense of Behavior: The Meaning of Control,* New Canaan, Benchmark.

Rosenthal, R. and Jacobson, L. (1968) *Pygmalion in the Classroom: Teacher Expectation and Pupils' Intellectual Development,* New York, Holt, Rinehart & Winston.

Rosenthal, R. and Lawson, R. (1964) 'A longitudinal study of the effects of experimenter bias on the operant learning of laboratory rats', *Journal of Psychiatric Research,* vol. 2, no. 2, pp. 61–72.

Surprising Studies of Visual Awareness (2003) vol. 1 (DVD). Champaign, Viscog Productions, Inc.

Taylor, J. B. (2008a) *My Stroke of Insight.* Youtube video, added by TED (Online). Available at www.youtube.com/watch?v=UyyjU8fzEYU (Accessed 17 January 2019).

Taylor, J. B. (2008b) *My Stroke of Insight: A Brain Scientist's Personal Journey,* New York, Viking.

Tolle, E. (2016) *The Power of Now: A Guide to Spiritual Enlightenment,* London, Yellow Kite.

Tzu, L. (2013) *Tao Te Ching: An Illustrated Journey* (trans. S. Mitchell), London, Frances Lincoln Limited.

Wegner, D. (1989) *White Bears and Other Unwanted Thoughts: Suppression, Obsession, and the Psychology of Mental Control,* New York, Viking/Penguin.

Wells, S. and Taylor, G. (eds) (2005) *William Shakespeare: The*

Complete Works, Oxford, Oxford University Press.

Wright, F. L. (1954) *The Natural House*, New York, Horizon Press.

BOOKS

SPIRITUALITY

O is a symbol of the world, of oneness and unity; this eye represents knowledge and insight. We publish titles on general spirituality and living a spiritual life. We aim to inform and help you on your own journey in this life.

If you have enjoyed this book, why not tell other readers by posting a review on your preferred book site?

Recent bestsellers from O-Books are:

Heart of Tantric Sex
Diana Richardson
Revealing Eastern secrets of deep love and intimacy to Western couples.
Paperback: 978-1-90381-637-0 ebook: 978-1-84694-637-0

Crystal Prescriptions
The A-Z guide to over 1,200 symptoms and their healing crystals
Judy Hall
The first in the popular series of eight books, this handy little guide is packed as tight as a pill-bottle with crystal remedies for ailments.
Paperback: 978-1-90504-740-6 ebook: 978-1-84694-629-5

Take Me To Truth
Undoing the Ego
Nouk Sanchez, Tomas Vieira
The best-selling step-by-step book on shedding the Ego, using the
teachings of *A Course In Miracles*.
Paperback: 978-1-84694-050-7 ebook: 978-1-84694-654-7

The 7 Myths about Love...Actually!
The Journey from your HEAD to the HEART of your SOUL
Mike George
Smashes all the myths about LOVE.
Paperback: 978-1-84694-288-4 ebook: 978-1-84694-682-0

The Holy Spirit's Interpretation of the New Testament
A Course in Understanding and Acceptance
Regina Dawn Akers
Following on from the strength of *A Course In Miracles*, NTI
teaches us how to experience the love and oneness of God.
Paperback: 978-1-84694-085-9 ebook: 978-1-78099-083-5

The Message of A Course In Miracles
A translation of the Text in plain language
Elizabeth A. Cronkhite
A translation of *A Course in Miracles* into plain, everyday
language for anyone seeking inner peace. The companion
volume, *Practicing A Course In Miracles*, offers practical lessons
and mentoring.
Paperback: 978-1-84694-319-5 ebook: 978-1-84694-642-4

Thinker's Guide to God
Peter Vardy
An introduction to key issues in the philosophy of religion.
Paperback: 978-1-90381-622-6

Your Simple Path
Find Happiness in every step
Ian Tucker
A guide to helping us reconnect with what is really important in
our lives.
Paperback: 978-1-78279-349-6 ebook: 978-1-78279-348-9

365 Days of Wisdom
Daily Messages To Inspire You Through The Year
Dadi Janki
Daily messages which cool the mind, warm the heart and guide
you along your journey.
Paperback: 978-1-84694-863-3 ebook: 978-1-84694-864-0

Body of Wisdom
Women's Spiritual Power and How it Serves
Hilary Hart
Bringing together the dreams and experiences of women across
the world with today's most visionary spiritual teachers.
Paperback: 978-1-78099-696-7 ebook: 978-1-78099-695-0

Dying to Be Free
From Enforced Secrecy to Near Death to True Transformation
Hannah Robinson
After an unexpected accident and near-death experience, Hannah
Robinson found herself radically transforming her life, while a
remarkable new insight altered her relationship with her father, a
practising Catholic priest.
Paperback: 978-1-78535-254-6 ebook: 978-1-78535-255-3

The Ecology of the Soul
A Manual of Peace, Power and Personal Growth for Real People
in the Real World
Aidan Walker
Balance your own inner Ecology of the Soul to regain your
natural state of peace, power and wellbeing.
Paperback: 978-1-78279-850-7 ebook: 978-1-78279-849-1

Not I, Not other than I
The Life and Teachings of Russel Williams
Steve Taylor, Russel Williams
The miraculous life and inspiring teachings of one of the World's
greatest living Sages.
Paperback: 978-1-78279-729-6 ebook: 978-1-78279-728-9

On the Other Side of Love
A woman's unconventional journey towards wisdom
Muriel Maufroy
When life has lost all meaning, what do you do?
Paperback: 978-1-78535-281-2 ebook: 978-1-78535-282-9

Practicing A Course In Miracles
A translation of the Workbook in plain language, with mentor's
notes
Elizabeth A. Cronkhite
The practical second and third volumes of The Plain-Language
A Course In Miracles.
Paperback: 978-1-84694-403-1 ebook: 978-1-78099-072-9

Quantum Bliss
The Quantum Mechanics of Happiness, Abundance, and Health
George S. Mentz
Quantum Bliss is the breakthrough summary of success and
spirituality secrets that customers have been waiting for.
Paperback: 978-1-78535-203-4 ebook: 978-1-78535-204-1

The Upside Down Mountain
Mags MacKean
A must-read for anyone weary of chasing success and happiness
– one woman's inspirational journey swapping the uphill slog for
the downhill slope.
Paperback: 978-1-78535-171-6 ebook: 978-1-78535-172-3

Your Personal Tuning Fork
The Endocrine System
Deborah Bates
Discover your body's health secret, the endocrine system, and
'twang' your way to sustainable health!
Paperback: 978-1-84694-503-8 ebook: 978-1-78099-697-4

Readers of ebooks can buy or view any of these bestsellers by
clicking on the live link in the title. Most titles are published
in paperback and as an ebook. Paperbacks are available in
traditional bookshops. Both print and ebook formats are
available online.

Find more titles and sign up to our readers' newsletter at
http://www.johnhuntpublishing.com/mind-body-spirit

Follow us on Facebook at https://www.facebook.com/OBooks/
and Twitter at https://twitter.com/obooks